Hoosier Farmers (1919-1999) Era of Change

A History Of Indiana Farm Bureau

Barbara Stahura

Published by
Indiana Farm Bureau, Inc., Indianapolis, Indiana

About The Author

Barbara Stahura is a freelance writer based in Evansville, Indiana. After six years of writing for a utility company, she began freelancing in January 1994. Her articles, essays, and poetry have been published in a variety of regional, national, and international publications, as well as online. She is co-editor and co-writer of *Just in Case: Dispatches from the Front Lines of the Y2K Crisis* and author of several military unit histories and county histories.

Turner Publishing Company
Publishers of America's History

Co-published by
Mark A. Thompson, Associate Publisher

For book publishing write to:
M.T. Publishing Company, Inc.
P.O. Box 6802
Evansville, Indiana 47719-6802

Pre-Press work by M.T. Publishing Company, Inc.
Graphic Designer: Elizabeth A. Dennis

Author: Barbara Stahura

Library of Congress Catalog
Card No. 99-75776

ISBN: 978-1-56311-526-4

Limited Edition

Contents

Introduction

Dear Members & Friends:

Hoosier Farmers. . . Era of Change traces our grassroots to global interests for the last 30 years. Our organization's history from the late 1960s to nearly 2000 is a whirlwind of adapting to agriculture's changing ways.

Farmer dedication to the ideals of their organization is quickly revealed as the pages are read. Working on behalf of farmer members, Farm Bureau has tirelessly and relentlessly worked for Indiana agriculture.

Our state organization has also added its clout on national issues. We have representation on the American Farm Bureau board of directors and many of our members serve on AFBF national advisory committees.

This book tells of the strong links between Farm Bureau, the Farm Bureau Cooperative, Farm Bureau Insurance and Producers Marketing Association...all valuable allies in a farmer's pursuit of excellence. We have also included our ties to extension, Purdue and Indiana's legislative and regulatory processes. They are an integral part of Indiana's agriculture.

These close working relationships and commitments have been necessary to ensure survival and success in all sectors of agriculture. Ironically, history does have a way of repeating itself. Our earlier history book, *Hoosier Farmers in a New Day*, documented our first 50 years. Our second, *Hoosier Farmers. . . Era of Change*, contains many similar issues.

Of course there are different twists and turns and the people, many times, are different. And the solutions this time around are probably far more sophisticated and complex and the rate of change is quicker. But the results are the same...a better future for agriculture and the organization that represents farmers and the agricultural community.

In the limited number of pages, we have painted a broad landscape of Farm Bureau's involvement in local, state and national issues. Even as the book went to the printers, many important events were taking place that deadlines prevented us from adding.

We (Farm Bureau) have been blessed with members willing to step forward and become involved. This book is dedicated to the many volunteers and farm leaders that have devoted countless hours and even lifetimes to Farm Bureau.

Thank you,

Harry Pearson
IFB president

Acknowledgment

No history book can ever record all the events in a limited number of pages. *The Hoosier Farmer* magazine was a tremendous resource during author Barbara Stahura's research on crucial events that helped shape Indiana Farm Bureau.

Many interviews were conducted with current and past officers. Many retired staff members along with co-op, insurance, and incorporated personnel were questioned to gather the different perspectives essential to writing our historical account.

We have relied quite heavily on photographs. Many of the names and faces you will, no doubt, recognize. One of the main themes throughout the book deals with the many complex issues that transcend state and national boundaries.

One constant throughout the document is the emphasis on the member and Farm Bureau's intense desire to maintain the economic and social viability of farmers.

Farm Bureau's successes go beyond our programs and policy positions. Farm Bureau is people...members...farmers...insureds. All have a role in the organization.

Hoosier Farmers. . . Era of Change is important because it reflects our interest in the member. Our programs are developed and driven by county member needs and concerns.

Farm Bureau and farmers are adapting to the era of rapid change. In its 80-some years of existence, Farm Bureau has continued to evolve to meet the challenges so necessary for tomorrow's agriculture... because of intense member loyalty and involvement.

To all that contributed to this history, we say thank you!

Thomas W. Asher (retired)
Information & Public Relations Division

Ear corn was the main course for most Indiana hogs that roamed and rooted in pastures and harvested fields in the days before confined feeding buildings were developed. Photo from the early 1940s.

Prologue
From The 1920s Through The 1960s

(This prologue is a brief summary of the last history of
the Indiana Farm Bureau, *Hoosiers Farmers in a New Day,*
written by Edna Moore Colby and published in 1968.)

In the first years after "the war to end all wars" — World War I — farmers throughout the United States felt as though they were waging their own war merely to survive. While many sectors of the economy flourished, with industry in particular enjoying boom times, farming was more difficult than ever. Fledgling labor and trade unions were gaining strength and offering political clout to many industrial workers, but farmers had no such protection. Even though the country could not survive without the farmers who produce the food everyone needs, farmers had no social recognition and received little respect for their efforts. In fact, after being hailed as heroes throughout the war for boosting production, farmers in the immediate post-war years were condemned as profiteers when, due to changing economic conditions, the price of food skyrocketed.

One of the great difficulties of being a farmer during these times was that individual farmers had no control over the prices they received for their products. Since they were not organized into a group that could put pressure on the market in any way, they were at the mercy of the buyers, who, of course, aimed to pay the lowest possible price. Furthermore, as prices to the farmers declined, the economy of the times meant they had to pay steeply rising prices for the supplies and equipment they needed for their livelihoods.

Another problem came about as a direct result of the war. Millions of young men who had been to Europe, who had literally left the farm, were not interested in going back to live in rural areas. The country's total farm population took a nose-dive in the early 1920s as these young men decided to make their mark in the cities, rather than on the farms where they had grown up. This exodus created a severe manpower shortage that greatly increased the workload for those who remained and also required the purchase of expensive new machinery to do the work of the missing family members. No matter what they did, it seemed, farmers could not win.

Even though farmers had created associations and organizations, like the Grange, in earlier decades, these groups did not provide the political power and protection that a combined, national effort could offer. Therefore, when

Hundreds of farmers marched to the Statehouse in Indianapolis to show their support for a gross income tax in 1933.

the American Farm Bureau Federation began to form, many farmers were eager to join. Hoosier farmers were among the first to organize, and Indiana was the first state to join. "Equality for agriculture" became the demand of the Indiana Federation of Farmers' Associations, later to be known as the Indiana Farm Bureau, Inc. In 1919, they declared their purpose in these words: "An organization of the farmers, by the farmers, to protect the interests of farmers; and by education, legislation and other honorable means, to promote the largest good for all the people."

At a meeting in Indianapolis in April 1919, the new federation issued a declaration of principles that listed their three reasons for organizing: 1. For mutual protection as any other class of workers and producers; 2. To promote farm home betterment and the general interest and welfare of communities; and 3. To preserve and extend our civil and religious institutions.

In one of the federation's first actions, taken at this same meeting, members called on Congress to stabilize food prices.

In this way, Indiana farmers began the long process of unifying with each other for their mutual good and protection.

IFB And Purdue Extension Service

One organization from which farmers could logically expect support for their new federation was the Cooperative Extension Service, established a decade before the Indiana Federation of Farmers' Associations came into existence. However, the two groups at first had a rocky time as they searched for a way to work together.

Marion Stackhouse, left, IFB president, congratulated Mauri Williamson, the recipient of the 1977 Frederick Hovde award of excellence in education service to rural people of Indiana. Presented during the state convention, Williamson was accompanied by his wife, June. Williamson was executive secretary of the Purdue Agricultural Alumni Association and for 24 years supervised, improved and expanded Ag Alumni Association activities at Purdue and throughout Indiana.

The Extension Service had not yet been fully funded in Indiana, where counties had to establish financial support for the program. By state law, the county board of education had to approve the candidates for the job of extension agent. However, the problem was that many school boards, composed of township trustees and the county superintendent of schools, were not eager to spend money for the benefit of farmers, not realizing that improvement in the rural economy would also benefit urban dwellers.

At the same time, agricultural administrators at Purdue University, which was highly involved in the promotion of the Extension Service, believed that the new Farm Bureau was an ideal avenue for promotion of the service. They were eager to join forces. However, even though some county divisions of the Indiana Farm Bureau intended to work closely with the Extension Service, others believed that this kind of connection would severely limit the fledging organization. Eventually, the two groups forged a strong relationship, and the IFB continues to independently support the Extension Service around the state.

IFB Women's Department

Not all farmers are male; women are also an essential part of farm families. Although the Indiana Federation of Farmers' Associations realized this, the federation formed at a time when women were not yet recognized as equal partners in society as a whole. Furthermore, according to *Hoosiers Farmers in a New Day,* "farmers psychologically were especially backward in according equal rights to women." Therefore, not until two years after the 1919 formation of the group were women allowed in as active participants. The farm women's cause was given a boost by the passage in 1920 of the Nineteenth Amendment to the Constitution that gave women the right to vote.

Women's participation finally began to take shape in March 1922, when the federation's first president, John G. Brown, called a state meeting to outline a program for federation women. He said, "We hope it may be generally known that women have the same rights and privileges to membership in the Federation of Farmers' Associations as men. There are great fields now open for the work of women... We are planning to take up sanitation and other helpful activities to promote and protect the farm home and community... Women are urged to join the Federation on the same terms as men, as we need their help and they need the help of men in this great co-operative movement."

Indiana Governor Otis Bowen, M.D., signed a Farm-City Festival Day proclamation as part of events sponsored by IFB's Women's Committee. Taking part was the 1979 executive women's committee, from left: Carol Hegel, Dist. 4; Dorothy Hon, Dist. 10; Bowen; Lois Gross, IFB Women's Committee chair; and Florence Walters, Dist. 3.

J. M. Rhodes proudly displays a town mileage marker to Gosport and promotes Farm Bureau membership in 1940.

The women's program began in what was then called the Social and Educational Department. It was at first headed by a man, L. A. Pittenger of Delaware County. As a former teacher, he was very concerned with rural school improvement. However, women began taking part at the very first meeting, held in March 1922, which was chaired by Edna Sewell. She was later named head of the women's department and then became chairman of home and community activities of the federation, a post she held for 16 years. In 1925, she became the first woman elected to the IFB board of directors and later moved into a national capacity.

After that meeting, it was still several years before the women's department became more than an offshoot of the federation. Over the decades since then, the women's department has expanded its focus from purely local issues to state, national, and international affairs.

Cooperatives Proliferate

Even before the federation was formed, Indiana farmers had many complaints and concerns about the marketing of livestock. Many times, livestock were ill-treated at stockyards and shipping points, causing them harm and even death, which meant that the farmers who had raised them lost their investment. In addition, farmers often had difficulty getting their animals to market at all, having to drive them on foot or load them into trucks, wagons, or more rarely, rail cars.

The new federation encouraged farmers to form local shipping associations. Within these associations, farmers would gather their livestock at a central point from where they would be either shipped to a terminal or sold to a local buyer.

The biggest benefit of this effort was to ease the transportation problem. Farmers could combine their shipments and share transportation costs before selling their livestock to the highest bidder at the terminal. Unfortunately, this had little effect on the market, where prices could swing wildly.

Farmers soon realized they could take more control of the sale part of the process, and they formed an organization to do so. The Indianapolis Producers' Commission Agency opened its doors on May 15, 1922, under the management of D. L. Swanson. It would later be re-named the Producers Marketing Association and have a long history. This agency would receive livestock on consignment, withhold operating expenses as its commission, and return the remainder of the receipts to the farmer. Its slogan was "In the Hands of a Friend from Beginning to End." In its first seven months of operation, the agency handled $1 million worth of livestock.

During its first four years, PMA refunded over $100,000 to Indiana farmers and stopped existing commission firms from raising their charges by up to

$15 a carload, which saved farmers $600,000 during that time. PMA was also able to bring about significant increases in the price of hogs, lambs, and sheep.

As it became more common to ship by truck and rail, the shipping associations became outmoded. But the Producers Marketing Association kept pace with change, following as packers moved to the country to buy livestock at the farm.

By the 1960s, the Producers' Co-operative was offering breeding and feeder livestock to farmers, as well as working with the Indiana Farm Bureau Co-operative Association in a feeder pig program. The PMA was then ranked among the largest hog marketing associations in the United States, having joined in May 1958 with the Columbus, Ohio, Producers' Association to form the Eastern Order Buyers, Inc., a jointly-owned hog sales agency for the two associations.

Wool producers also decided to work cooperatively and began selling their wool to the Ohio Wool and Sheep Growers' Association in 1921. They pooled their product and signed contracts that helped them all make a better profit. In 1926, the Indiana Wool Growers Association was incorporated. It operated independently until 1947, when it merged with the Indiana Farm Bureau Co-operative Association.

Not all early experiments with cooperatives were successful, however. Two that failed were the onion and tomato co-ops.

The Indiana Farm Bureau Onion Exchange was established in 1920. At first, they had great success, expanding sales from nine markets to 88 markets in 23 states. Four years later, they decided to act as their own selling agency. Unfortunately, lack of size and experience meant they could not effectively influence the onion market. Soon thereafter, the Onion Exchange failed.

In 1924, the Indiana Canning Crops Exchange was created, at first dealing primarily with tomatoes. They were very successful in their efforts, with prices to farmers jumping almost immediately. However, in 1925, canners were paying $4 more per ton than they had two years earlier, and therefore many did not abide by their contracts with the Canning Crops Exchange. Since the co-op was left with an excess of tomatoes, they built 18 canning plants around the state. These plants were most successful in remote areas with no large towns or railroads nearby. Unfortunately, the exchange failed to create a plan for selling what they canned. Eventually, this co-op failed because the farmers ended up with hundreds of tons of tomatoes and no market.

The demise of both of these co-ops pointed out a serious problem faced by the Indiana Farm Bureau: Farmers were not typically good marketers of their own products and, as a group, could not make up their mind about how far they should move into marketing. Additionally, rugged individualism was

In the 1940s and 1950s nearly every farm had a flock of chickens. These Farm Bureau Co-op chicks were delivered with a note on the shipping label, "chicks born 2 p.m., August 17, 1948." Sunday fried chicken dinners and "egg money" for household necessities were long standing traditions.

Carroll County Farm Bureau members met in Delphi in 1949 to plan membership activities for the coming year.

the order of the day, and farmers were not accustomed to banding together for their common good. It would take a long process of education for them to realize this and then act upon it.

Dairy cooperatives were more successful. In the early 1920s, the quality of dairy products delivered to groceries was uneven, and the cooperatives aimed to eliminate this problem. In 1921, the Indiana Dairy Marketing Association was incorporated.

The association created more local cream stations, where farmers could bring their cream for sale. However, many farmers considered dairying only a sideline, so the volume in some areas was insufficient. They also had little say in the operation of the stations, many of which were not wisely located, so they had little interest in their success. As a result, the association was not very effective in its early years.

However, as the demand for more dairy products grew, regional manufacturing and bargaining co-ops were established. Over the years, these included Mid-West Producers Creameries, Inc., in South Bend; Farmers Marketing Association in Columbus; Pure-Milk Association of Chicago, which served northwestern Indiana; Wayne Co-operative Milk Producers in Fort Wayne; Central Indiana Dairymen's Association in Indianapolis; Vigo County Milk Producers in Terre Haute; and Co-operative Pure Milk Association in Cincinnati, which handled the milk of southeastern Indiana dairy farmers.

Grain farmers were not to be left out of the move to cooperatives. Just prior to 1920, a scandal erupted regarding how the Chicago Board of Trade, the country's center of grain marketing, was exploiting the grain farmers. To protect themselves from this kind of treatment, Hoosier grain growers formed the Indiana Grain Dealers' Association in 1920. The small grain farmers and grain handlers banded together to gain market strength. Soon afterwards, they joined with the federation and the Indiana Grange to create the Federated Marketing Service.

In 1926, grain producers in Indiana, Ohio, and Illinois created a bargaining group called the Central Growers Association. The Hoosier portion of the group was called the Indiana Grain Growers' Association, headquartered in the Indiana Farm Bureau headquarters in Indianapolis. However, in 1938, IFB officers decided to organize the grain business into a cooperative, which they named the Indiana Grain Cooperative. Its first manager was M. D. Guild of Pulaski County. It later merged with the Indiana Farm Bureau Cooperative Association in 1950, in part because the IFBCA could more easily maintain a flow of adequate capital. All these efforts worked as farmers began to learn how to effectively market their products. By the late 1960s, despite the gigantic increase in handling costs, the handling margin for grain was about one-third what it was when farmers began their efforts of improve grain marketing.

The Indiana Farm Bureau And Its Services Continue To Grow

In 1926, the Federated Marketing Service disbanded after the Grange and the Grain Dealers' Association pulled out. When IFB leaders decided to create a better buying and selling program for its members, they reorganized the marketing service. It later came to be called the Indiana Farm Bureau Cooperative Association. I. H. Hull was named manager. Under his guidance, the IFBCA generated more than $2 million in annual business within its first two years. (By the late 1960s, it was the largest farmer-owned cooperative in the country, doing business in a state.)

The role of the IFBCA was to purchase and sell many of the products that farmers needed to do their jobs. To that end, the association bought oil wells and became a petroleum producer. It owned a seed plant and manufactured plant food, and to control costs further it began investing in plant food ingredients. The IFBCA even sold farm machinery, going so far as to manufacture a better farm tractor with rubber tires and a high compression motor for about 20 years. The association also conducted farm research.

The federation had an official magazine from its start in 1919. In May of that year, they contracted for "no less than 25,000 copies" of the magazine, *The Organized Farmer*, later to be called *The Hoosier Farmer*. This huge order was based solely on faith, since there was no certainty at the time that this many subscriptions could be sold.

The magazine's first editor, W. H. Hickman, wrote the following in his editorial in the first issue, distributed in June 1919. It reflects the philosophy that the Indiana Farm Bureau continues to espouse today:

> We are not out for class legislation, but a square deal between the three general classes—producers, distributors, and consumers. We will not go so far as some will advise, and probably go further than the opinions of others; but we would say to our progressives and conservatives give us a season of "Watchful Waiting." The devil has two methods of dealing with men and instruments of public opinion. He holds back these forces in the good old ways of our fathers as long as possible, but when the leaven of reform will be no longer restrained, he boosts reformers and instruments of reform to make them go too fast and too far. We shall go ahead with our job, studying the problems that we are sure to meet, and that we are in the field to meet, but not losing touch with the multitudes of men and women going our way.

As the IFB matured, the magazine circulation numbers continued to grow, and for many years, it was printed by independent printers. Then, in 1943, a printing plant in Spencer, Indiana, came available through bankruptcy proceedings. Through equal investments, Indiana Farm Bureau, Indiana Farm Bureau Co-operative Association, and Farm Bureau Mutual Insurance Association Company of Indiana purchased the plant as a cooperative and renamed it Farm Bureau Printing Corporation. In 1950, it reincorporated as a for-profit business. The plant eventually printed 16 periodicals in addition to *The Hoosier Farmer.* Later, the printing plant was sold and printing was once again contracted out.

The Hoosier Travel Service incorporated as an IFB affiliate in 1948, brought about by an increasing interest in travel among Indiana farm families. Glenn Sample was a key player in its creation. During its 18 years of operation, 7,000 people took advantage of its services to travel throughout North America, and to Europe, Israel, Hawaii, Japan, Hong Kong, New Zealand, Australia, and Central and South America. The travel service was sold to an independent operator in 1966 and discontinued as an IFB affiliate.

In 1946, the IFB board of directors opened three cooperative food stores, called the Producers' & Consumers' Family Food Stores, in Lebanon, Greensburg, and Veedersburg. The IFB, the Indiana Farm Bureau Co-operative Association, and the Producers Marketing Association bought the voting stock, while farmers and co-ops purchased the non-voting, preferred stock. However, the farmers soon saw they could not compete with the newly-emerging chain grocery stores, and the stores were closed.

Farm Bureau Insurance Created To Meet Farm Needs

In the early 1920s, the IFB agreed to act as agent for the fledgling State Farm Mutual Insurance Co., of Bloomington, Illinois. State Farm was thus able to provide for the insurance needs of Hoosier farmers, who were often underinsured and frequently fell economic victim to weather and accident. With its limited funds at the time, the IFB did not believe it could establish its own insurance company.

State Farm's business grew rapidly, and the IFB received $30,000 in annual commissions. However, surveys done by IFBCA leaders determined in the early 1930s that Indiana farmers could establish their own insurance

This Producers' and Consumers' Family Food Store in Veedersburg was in operation in 1946.

company. In 1934, the issue came to a showdown between those IFB members and officials for and those against the creation of such a company. It was settled at the 1934 IFB convention, with the "pro" faction emerging victorious.

As a result, in February 1935, the Farm Bureau Mutual Insurance Company was licensed to sell automobile insurance. In 1946, a new company was created to provide tornado and fire insurance, and it merged with the Mutual Insurance Company two years later.

The Hoosier Farm Bureau Life Insurance Company was established in 1937 as a legal reserve mutual company. Thanks to a most enthusiastic response, this company was able to expand in later years and offer medical insurance as well.

For many years, Indiana Farm Bureau's conventon facilities were in the Murat Temple. The marquee greeted Bureau members to the November annual meeting in 1951.

Over the years, other insurance companies were formed under the IFB umbrella, and some were disbanded or merged with others. Overall, however, the insurance companies of the Indiana Farm Bureau have been very successful and today continue to cover the insurance needs of thousands of Hoosier farm families.

Electricity Comes To The Farm

Long after Indiana cities were blessed with electricity, most rural areas were still left literally in the dark. It's difficult to imagine today the hardships farm families suffered without the benefit of electricity. Their daytime work was made more difficult and time-consuming by the lack of electricity, and they could not easily work after dark.

However, in 1936, the Indiana General Assembly passed the State Rural Electrification Act, which authorized the development of the Rural Electric Membership Cooperatives. This plan allowed rural dwellers to band together in cooperatives to raise money and make loans to bring electricity to their areas.

In the same year, the Rural Electrification Association made available federal funds for the construction of rural electric distribution facilities, which gave IFBCA leaders, working with the IFB, the impetus it needed to do the original planning and direct the electrification of Indiana farms.

Their solicitors visited farms all over the state, and they found that farmers did not need much encouragement to contribute to the fund that would provide them with electricity. At one point, the IFBCA had $87,000 invested in organization work for the REMCs.

By 1937, electric distribution lines had been strung to 30,000 rural homes, and in four more years, 50,000 Hoosier farm homes had electricity. The work continued until all farms were so blessed.

In 1967, a division of the Indiana Statewide Rural Electric Cooperative, called Hoosier Energy Division, constructed a power plant near Petersburg. Several REMCs cooperated to build the plant with a Rural Electrification Association loan.

IFB And Legislation

From the beginning, the IFB turned to the legislature for help with farm-related problems. The first IFB-sponsored bill was passed by the Indiana General Assembly in 1921 — an act that allowed livestock to be transported to the Indianapolis stockyards and market via interurban rail cars.

Other early concerns the IFB took to the legislature included proposals for broadening the tax base, practicing strict economy in state government, the establishment of purity standards for seeds, and the busing of rural high school students to schools, which were often far away from their homes.

In 1922, the Farm Bureau named a board of directors to handle the upcoming legislative season. This was a precursor to the establishment of a political action committee, or federal PAC, in the 1980s.

By the next year, state legislators knew the IFB was a force to be reckoned with. Indiana farmers were finally making themselves heard on a statewide level. In the years to come, they would play an increasing role in state lawmaking. Later, they would also make their mark in national and international affairs as well. Their strength came from their unity as well as their conviction that farmers play a crucial role in the economy not only of the nation but of the world.

Better Marketing Strategies

By the late 1950s, farmers around the country began to see the need for developing a strong bargaining organization to represent them during the sale of their products. In 1960, the American Farm Bureau established the American Agricultural Marketing Association; the next year, the IFB created their affiliated Indiana Agricultural Marketing Association. Its goal was to improve marketing conditions and prices to Hoosier farmers.

✻ ✻ ✻ ✻ ✻

Edna Moore Colby wrote her history of the Indiana Farm Bureau, Hoosier Farmers in a New Day, *at the end of the 1960s, which was a tumultuous time in the United States. The decade heralded the beginning of massive societal changes that have never stopped; indeed, even to the turn of the 21st century, these changes have done nothing but accelerate. Since farming does not exist in a vacuum, the world of Indiana agriculture also has undergone considerable change in the last 30 years—and, necessarily, so has the Indiana Farm Bureau. Colby foreshadowed this in her book when she wrote of the IFB: "A great body of endeavor has gone into its development, which will not end so long as the program shifts to meet the needs of the people on the land."*

Since the time when Colby wrote her history, the number of "the people on the land," has decreased drastically; only a minuscule portion of the population still farms, unlike the days when the IFB was founded and half the population were farmers. Farmers need representation more than ever before, and the Indiana Farm Bureau has not faltered in its support. Its challenges at the turn of the 20th century are much different than when it began. Today, at the dawn of the new millennium, the challenge is to meet a growing diversity of member needs while remaining a strong organization as the number of Hoosier farmers continues to decrease. This new history will pick up where Colby's left off.

Producers Marketing Association was one of the largest volume sellers of fed cattle at the Indianapolis Livestock Market. The picture was taken in 1962.

Richard Nixon was the featured speaker at the 1969 American Farm Bureau's 50th birthday celebration. To the left was AFBF President, Charles Schuman.

Chapter One
Farm Bill And Labor Unrest

In 1969, the Indiana Farm Bureau had been in existence for 50 years. During their first half-century together, IFB members had learned a great deal about the business of marketing their products, working within the legislative process, and banding together when necessary for their common good. They had forged a successful organization that had given them a strong presence and voice in Indiana agriculture. To honor all these accomplishments, they planned a golden anniversary celebration that would bring them together in Indianapolis.

Two years earlier, in the fall of 1967, George Doup, IFB president, had appointed a committee to plan the event. The eight people that made up the committee represented the four major organizations under the IFB umbrella at the time; two members each came from Indiana Farm Bureau, Inc., Farm Bureau Insurance, Producers Marketing Association, and Farm Bureau Co-op. Doup appointed Estel Callahan, IFB education director, as committee chairman.

From the start, the plan was to bring 10,000 IFB members from all 92 Indiana counties to celebrate the occasion at the Indiana State Fairgrounds in Indianapolis. After much study, the committee settled on a date of March 19, 1969. Callahan recalled, "Two things did concern us. The cattle barn (where the dinner was to be held) wasn't heated—this was March, mind you—and the roof of the cattle barn was leaking in many spots at that time. After a lot of preparation, I finally decided the sun was going to shine, it was going to be dry, it wasn't going to be too cold—and that's the way it turned out."

Over the course of two years, the committee planned this event much like generals plan a major battle. Their major challenge was the prompt feeding of 10,000 people, who would be seated at literally two miles of tables. The committee decided to use 20 serving lines to serve a dinner of smoked pork loin on buns, baked beans, cole slaw, potato chips, ice cream sundae cups, and milk and coffee—at a cost of $1.22 per person. Everything was so well organized that everyone was served in an incredible 40 minutes! (The Indiana Board of Health was so impressed with the event's organization, they filmed the serving of the meal to use as a training film for other groups planning to serve large groups.)

After the dinner, those in attendance moved to the State Fair Coliseum and heard speeches from the new Secretary of Agriculture, Clifford M. Hardin, and Earl Butz, then a dean of Purdue University and later to be secretary of Agriculture. They were entertained by country signing star Eddy Arnold. All in all, the anniversary celebration was a rousing success.

Later, Callahan wrote a synopsis of the event and all the planning that led up to it. He concluded by saying, "Any success March 19, 1969 was due to the four organizations that wanted it to be a big success, a committee that knew how to plan and execute a plan, staff people of all levels who willingly helped, and most of all to members in the counties who were willing to participate and help celebrate the Golden Anniversary of their Farm Organization."

Except for the anniversary celebration, 1969 was a typical year for the Indiana Farm Bureau and its related organizations. Work continued on all fronts as it had for decades.

On March 20, 1969, the Indiana Farm Bureau Cooperative Association (IFBCA) unveiled its new Central Feed Mill and Central Laboratory in Indianapolis. Co-op members who attended the annual meeting took a tour of the facility, which held some of the most modern feed mill equipment in the world at the time. The mill could produce 200 tons of supplements for swine and beef in an eight-hour shift.

The lab handled the research and quality control functions required by the cooperative system. Among the functions the lab handled were soil analysis, forage testing, and plant tissue testing. It also tested raw materials and finished products produced by the Co-op for quality control.

Central Feed Mill was the second of three planned Indiana mills. The first was already operational in Loogootee, and the third was to be built near Rochester.

Another kind of technology was beginning to play a new role in the life of Indiana farmers. *The Hoosier Farmer* stated,

> A typical Indiana farm is more than just a home; it is really a small factory and as such the farmer must have clear concise records upon which to base decisions. In the last 30 years, capital investment has increased more than eight times; the value of productive farm assets has soared to more than 450 per cent of what it was just 20 years ago. And, by 1980, investments in agriculture will likely increase another 50 per cent. (November 1969)

Some 10,000 Indiana Farm Bureau members and guests were fed during the organization's 50th birthday celebration. The event was held at the Indiana State Fairgrounds. The meal was served in the Cattle Barn in 1969.

Entertaining the 50th birthday celebration crowd of 10,000 was country singer Eddy Arnold. Backstage he visited with from left: Lois Gross, Martha Doup, Estel Callahan and George Doup.

This meant that concise record keeping on the farm was becoming more crucial than ever. To assist its farm members, the IFB created an electronic data processing (EDP) system that helped with money management decisions. By 1969, 200 Hoosier farm families had signed up for this service.

As part of this service, participating farmers received regular cash-flow reports, journal listings of income and expenses, a complete farm ledger, and expenses with monthly and year-end totals. In addition, they received annual reports including a detailed depreciation schedule, a capital gains and losses report, investment credit summary, and annual inventory of grain, feed, supplies and livestock.

If farmers chose, they could also receive a farm business analysis that included returns for management, labor, return per $100 of feed, power and equipment costs per crop acre, and equipment investment per acre. Using this analysis, they could "easily determine which operation is the most profitable and if one operation is capable of carrying another. A farmer can see where to make capital investments or operational improvements," J. Joseph Edwards, IFB Service Co. director, told *The Hoosier Farmer.*

During 1969, legislative issues were once again at the forefront of the IFB workload. Pointing out that membership had reached a high point of 158,000, IFB President George Doup wrote in the January issue of *The Hoosier Farmer* that "Indiana Farm Bureau has entered this state legislative year with all stops pulled." Property tax reform and change in the state's time zones were on the list of legislative priorities, and Indiana farmers wanted to make sure their views were heard. Doup encouraged all IFB members to stay informed about these and other legislative issues so they might be ready for "instant action" with their own legislators if the need arose during the session, which ran until March 11.

As usual during the General Assembly session, the IFB legislative team was on the scene in Indianapolis. Led by Hollys E. Moon, the team kept up a brisk, even exhausting pace as they kept track of what was happening with more than 1,800 bills and resolutions. A major part of their task was to research the possible affects that hundreds of these bills could have on farmers. They also kept the IFB leadership informed and presented testimony to legislators, many of whom were from urban areas and did not have a first-hand understanding of the problems faced by farmers—and of the additional problems new laws might present to them.

The Hoosier Farmer praised the results of the 1969 IFB lobbying efforts as "every bit as good if not better than it has been in recent sessions." In many areas, farmers fared well with new legislation, including health and safety, natural resources, and commodity and marketing issues.

One piece of legislation strongly endorsed by the IFB did pass in the 1969 session—a bill putting most of Indiana on Eastern Standard Time. The organization had been pushing for this since 1919, when minutes of a board meeting resolved "that the Indiana Federation of Farmers Association instruct its officers to devise plans and do all within their power to have the present daylight saving law repealed."

Early in 1968, the Department of Transportation had declared that most of Indiana would be placed in the Eastern Standard Time Zone, which, without the intervention of the state General Assembly, would mean that during the summer, Hoosiers would have to observe Daylight Saving Time as well as Eastern Standard. The IFB filed a suit in U.S. District Court to enjoin the Department of Transportation from enforcing this change until a thorough study could be made of the effects the change would have on farmers and other businesses. Doup said this action was necessary because the time change "will hit us at the most crucial time in our farming session. Our already delicately-balanced farming business will be confronted with disrupted and damaged lines of farm supply and service; and vitally important markets will undoubtedly be disrupted, confused and depressed. Farmers just can't stand this kind of a jolt."

Thanks to this action by the IFB, the change was held off until the 1969 session of the General Assembly. However, in an action the IFB called "inexplainable," Governor Edgar Whitcomb vetoed the bill mandating the time zone change. Not until the 1971 legislative session did the lawmakers override the veto. The new law moved the dividing line between Central Time and Eastern Standard Time eastward to the Indiana-Ohio border, instead of down the middle of Indiana. Only a few counties in predominantly urban areas were exempt from this change and remained on Central Daylight Saving Time, setting clocks ahead in the spring and back in the fall.

However, in one major area where the IFB team worked very hard for change, the General Assembly took no action. Despite touting this as the most important issue of the session, the lawmakers made no changes to Indiana property tax laws, which the IFB had long maintained were unfair to farmers.

As would become apparent by June of 1969, when property tax assessments were sent out, Indiana farmers sorely needed tax reform. In the eight years since the last assessment, both land values and building costs had increased sharply, but net farm income hadn't kept pace. This meant farmers faced substantially higher tax rates with less income from which to pay them.

The IFB worked with the State Tax Board to encourage them to keep the new land value figures at reasonable rates. When the board set an increase estimated between 25 percent and 33-1/3 percent, the IFB maintained that property tax rates had to be sufficiently lowered to take these higher assess-

The traditional Indiana Breakfast was held during the 1969 AFBF Convention at the Mayflower Hotel in Chicago December 9. Congressional representatives and county Farm Bureau delegates were recognized. Among those at the head table were from left: U.S. Representative Earl Landgrebe; U.S. Senator Birch Bayh; Vance Denny, IFB treasurer; U.S. Senator Vance Hartke; and Martha Doup. IFB president George Doup is at the podium.

ment values into account. The fight over what George Doup called "the Number One problem for the General Assembly in its next session" would in fact go on for years. Not until 1973 were significant changes in Indiana property tax law enacted (and even then, further changes would be introduced and fought over through the 1990s). For its part, the IFB remained steadfast in its desire to see fair changes made.

When the Farm Bureau organized in 1919, there was little concern about foreign markets for American food products. However, that outlook had changed dramatically in the ensuing 50 years. Foreign markets, especially for corn, soybeans, and wheat, had taken on a major role in the nation's agricultural production and in the economy, since the United States was the world's largest food producer and, now, exporter. In the late 1960s, Indiana farmers exported 20 percent of all row crop production they grew, and their soybean exports alone amounted to $85 million.

The IFB believed that these numbers could be improved. In its 1969 Farm Bureau Policy, the section on "Expansion of Export Markets" explicitly states,

"Farm Bureau should continue to promote a trade development program for the sale of agricultural products abroad. Export opportunities should be explored in an effort to expand international trade."

Unfortunately, American farmers often had to battle with their own government to get a fair shake in foreign markets. When Congress ratified the International Wheat Trade Convention in 1968, the IFB protested because it would limit, rather than expand, foreign markets for soft winter wheat, which was a large crop in Indiana. George Doup commented, "...it seems obvious that we must be free to compete for world markets if we are to continue producing at the present or an expanding rate because the demand in this country is relatively inelastic. We will continue to be burdened with surpluses and low prices if export sales are not expanded."

He predicted that wheat exports and prices would drop if the convention was put into effect—which is exactly what happened. Several countries then decided to not abide by the convention. Indiana wheat farmers were hit hard. Doup once again called for congressional action.

During this time, the IFB continued pursuing its own avenues to foreign markets, including sending representatives to meet with agricultural and marketing experts in Europe. Marion Stackhouse, then director of the IFB commodity department, traveled there for three weeks in 1969 to study the agricultural markets. He visited Spain's largest soybean crusher and several hog producers, Italian cattle traders and soybean importers, German trade representatives, and the headquarters of the European Economic Community in Belgium.

His conclusion at the end of the three weeks? "Yes, there is certainly a great potential market in Europe," he said. "But it's going to take a lot of work to develop it." He later spoke to the Louisville (Kentucky) Producers Livestock Marketing Association and said that Hoosier farmers could compete for world markets if they work through organizations such as Producers Marketing Association and the grain cooperatives.

Along with protesting ratification of the International Wheat Trade Convention, the IFB was also calling for changes in the Food and Agricultural Act of 1965. The U. S. Department of Agriculture said government control of wheat, feed grain, and cotton under this act had helped significantly to reduce surpluses, which the USDA viewed as a positive step. The IFB disagreed with that statement, saying through *The Hoosier Farmer* that "the depletion of feed grain surpluses under Secretary [Orville] Freeman was due largely to increased utilization and not the government control program."

The magazine article continued:

> There is nothing on record to show that supply-management by government has ever really been effective in adjusting produc-

tion to market demand...The sooner the government wheat, feed grain and cotton control programs are phased out and the market system is allowed to operate, the sooner will farmers have a chance to adjust production to market needs and get higher net incomes. (May 1969)

Furthermore, the 1965 act had caused low farm prices for wheat, feed grains, and cotton at a taxpayer expense of $7 billion, as well as a call for limitation of farm payments—nothing that farmers appreciated yet all of which they had predicted.

Since the 1965 act was to expire in 1970, the American Farm Bureau drew up a proposed Agricultural Act of 1969. This bill proposed the gradual switch from a government-controlled system to a market-driven one and the phasing out of quotas and allotments, to be completed by 1975; the retirement of 50 million acres to keep production in line with demand; the maintenance of some price support loans at levels that would rarely cause the government to take title to the commodities and at rates that would not break the market; and loans for those farmers who wished to retire or change occupations.

This plan, said the IFB, would mean higher prices for farmers and lower costs to taxpayers.

Later in the year, Secretary of Agriculture Clifford Hardin appeared before the House Committee on Agriculture to present his recommendations for a new farm bill. The Farm Bureau declared that it was "disappointed" with his suggestions, saying he wished to retain the same farm programs that had been causing problems for 30 years and which continued what the IFB called "socialized agriculture." *The Hoosier Farmer* called for quick action on the part of Congress, instead of

> ...fritter(ing) away even another year in make-work studies, politically-inspired so-called 'hearings,' and repetitious discussion. Our U. S. farm program problems need action, not more study! Farmers could be studied right into the poor house. (November 1969)

In late summer of 1970, the U. S. House of Representatives voted on a new farm bill, which would expire with the end of the 1973 crop year. It was not the one proposed by the Farm Bureau and in fact contained many of the same provisions as the 1965 farm program. Nevertheless, it was passed into law, and *The Hoosier Farmer* praised the eight Indiana Representatives who voted against it.

The weaknesses of the approach taken by both the 1965 and proposed 1970 farm programs became apparent, at least to Indiana farmers, when both a drought and Southern Leaf Blight hit the Hoosier corn crop. Some corn growers reported as much as a 50 percent loss, and statewide production was

6 percent below the previous year's total. The outcome of this short crop, said the IFB, proved its contention that the 1965 farm bill worked against farmers. When the corn price shot up in early September, the Commodity Credit Corporation put millions of bushels of stored corn up for sale, which brought the market price down again. Thus, farmers who could have been helped by the higher prices lost most of their profit. The IFB and sister state Farm Bureaus continued their call for passage of the new farm bill developed by the American Farm Bureau Federation.

Not all farm organizations agreed with the Farm Bureau's proposed changes to the farm bill. Thirty-two smaller farm, commodity, political, and farm business organizations wanted Congress to continue with what the IFB called "welfare" programs for farmers. In March 1970, a coalition of these groups formed the National Education Institute for Agriculture. As the IFB pointed out, most of the officers, board members, and executives of the NEIA were cotton and wheat producers who were also executives of processing companies in the South or West. The NEIA's purpose, according to the IFB, was

> ...to "educate" urban people on the value of farm legislation which will freeze farming into a public utility—controlled by the public, for the benefit of the public, and not necessarily for the financial benefit of farmers. (*The Hoosier Farmer*, May 1970.)

The IFB added, rather dryly, "This is not a new goal of many people in government circles."

The IFB remained firm that the AFBF's proposed legislation to phase out wheat and feed grain allotments and quotas over five years and a land retirement program that would allow farmers to adjust to an over-supplied market was the only way to take farmers off government welfare and put themselves back on a strong economic footing.

Across the country, another challenge to farmers had begun in California's Kern County two years earlier and threatened to spread across the country. Under the leadership of Cesar Chavez, California migrant grape pickers had created the United Farm Workers Union to protest the poor conditions and pay under which they said they were forced to work. They asked people sympathetic with their cause to boycott California table grapes. The boycott spread across the country, and by January 1969, major grocery stores in the Midwest were discontinuing the sale of grapes.

The Hoosier Farmer deplored the boycott, saying it was "a serious threat to the Hoosier farming business and to urban consumers." The main fear was that such a boycott would spread to other products and crops, depriving the farmer of income and the consumer of free choice. Believing that the union was forcing unwilling workers to join, *The Hoosier Farmer* declared that if this kind of situation was allowed to persist, "then there is no reason why other irresponsible unions could not do the same with workers who help grow corn, milk, soybeans, beef cattle, hogs, apples and other farm products. This is where the grape fight hits Hoosiers."

As a visible sign of protest against the boycott, attendees to the American Farm Bureau Federation convention received cups of grapes and small boxes of raisins, while the press room tables held bunches of grapes for snacking. The Farm Bureau could never be accused of being shy when its principles were at stake!

George Doup wholeheartedly agreed with the AFBF. At the 51st annual IFB convention in November 1969, he declared that perishable-product boycotts like the one against table grapes should be prohibited by law. He also maintained that government officials had no business encouraging lower food prices to the detriment of farmers—an excellent reminder to farmers about why banding together under the Farm Bureau banner to create a united voice was so crucial to their welfare.

During the next year the AFL-CIO organized the grape pickers. This action alarmed the Farm Bureau because the union vowed to gain collective bargaining for farm workers across the country. *The Hoosier Farmer* opined,

> Neither farmers nor consumers in general can long afford the luxury of having never-satisfied labor union leaders speaking for the farmer's workers. In almost every line of business, a month-long labor strike means only the month-long loss of income to the workers and the company. In farming, such a stoppage can mean a loss of the entire year's production of food. This is unfair, unreasonable, illegal, and unsafe for the country. Such strikes and boycotts lead only to higher food prices, lower farm income, and greater financial strength of union organizations. (September 1970)

Even though some California lettuce pickers were organized into competing unions and a lettuce boycott declared the next year, the declaration that all farm workers would some day be unionized did not happen. In 1971, grape growers in Arizona sued the United Farm Workers, saying the union violated the Sherman Anti-Trust Act. The AFBF supported this action.

As boycotts of grapes and lettuce continued for the next few years, so did the actions of the United Farm Workers, arriving eventually in Indiana. In May 1972, demonstrators appeared in front of the Allen County Farm Bureau-Farm Bureau Insurance office in Ft. Wayne. According to *The Hoosier Farmer*,

> This was an apparent boycott display and was a part of a nationwide action to attack and discredit Farm Bureau and Farm Bu-

More than 2,000 Farm Bureau members and guests registered for the 54th annual state convention held at the Murat Temple in Indianapolis.

Will Erwin, USDA deputy undersecretary for rural development, was a guest speaker at the 1972 state convention. Following his presentation he was interviewed by Gene Wilson, IFB Information & Public Relations Department.

reau affiliated service companies. The demonstrators presumably represented the forces of Cesar Chavez and the United Farm Workers Union. (June 1972)

The Ft. Wayne demonstration was probably an extension of a Chicago appearance by UFW members the previous week. There, the union members demanded that Farm Bureau stop supporting labor legislation that the UFW believed was unfair to agricultural workers. Of course, Farm Bureau did not capitulate to this ultimatum. As George Doup wrote,

> Farm Bureau is not anti-labor. Farm Bureau is not anti-labor unions. Farm Bureau is not unresponsive to the concerns of migrant or other farm workers. However, we must have "ground rules" under which labor unions and farmers can operate and this is what Farm Bureau is attempting to get. . . The boycott against Farm Bureau will fail because farmer's contentions are reasonable and fair. (June 1972)

During the summer of 1972, pro-UFW individuals attempted to trespass on the farms of some Indiana vegetable growers in an attempt to distribute material and encourage migrant workers to join the union. The IFB said such action called for "passage of farm legislation which will give protection to both the producer and the laborer."

By the late 1970s, attempts at farm worker unionization had spread to much of the nation, and their cause had caught the attention of many other

Indiana delegates to the 1972 AFBF convention in Chicago were: (l. to r.) Front row: Glenn W. Sample; Oris Bedenkop; Victor Burger, St. Joseph; Lois Gross; Elmo Ray; George Neff; and George Doup. Back row: John Clark, Steuben; Bill Shafer, Harrison; Burrell Rosenbaum, Montgomery; Alton Gordon, Rush; Floyd Engle, Adams; Warren Wheaton; and Wayne Hasselbring, White.

Gov. Edgar D. Whitcomb, signed a proclamation declaring February 13-19, 1972 as Hoosier Pork Week in honor of Indiana pork producers. (l. to r.) George Doup, IFB president; Ralph Bishop and Bill Nash, pork producers; Ken Kohls, Indiana Pork Producers Association; Marion Stackhouse, IFB Commodity Department; and George Pickering, IPP president.

groups. Also involved by this time, according to *The Hoosier Farmer*, were the National Association of Farmworker Organizations, which was an umbrella group of 120 smaller groups in association with the United Farm Workers; federally-funded Migrant Action Programs; and church, labor, and consumer groups.

The IFB in no way objected to the unionization of farm workers; its objection stemmed from the ways in which it was conducted and promoted, and from other related activities and alliances that unfairly affected farm income. These alliances carried over into "other major concerns of market agriculture," said IFB President Marion Stackhouse in *The Hoosier Farmer* of September 1977. He continued,

> Labor-allied "consumer groups" whose objective is to press for low food prices, even while encouraging high wage guarantees for the food unions, are a part of this alliance—which regards the organization of farm workers as a first step to get a hold on food market management. Recently, Ralph Nader, consumer advocate, states that, "This legislation (a consumer protection agency) is essential to establish a strong consumer voice within government for low prices..."

Increased organizational activity increases the risks of strikes at harvest and of boycott pressures to close off farm markets...

Many of these groups assisting do not realize that they are playing into the hands of organized labor to create a monopoly power over the entire nation's economy.

Let it be known now and forever, I am not against workers joining the union—for we, too, ask farmers to join our organization. It is not prudent, however, to sit by and see extensive abuses destroy the economy of our country!...

We need a strong labor force in the country, but we also need responsible labor and government activities.

The farm worker movement continued through the 1980s and 1990s, although not with the same fervor as in the 1970s.

In March 1969, while the IFB 50th anniversary celebration was going on at the State Fairgrounds, the Producers Marketing Association was holding its annual meeting. General Manager W. R. Cummins, general manager, told the PMA delegates, "If livestock producers are ever to solve their own marketing problems, their cooperatives must be large, efficient and progressive. They must be financially strong and able to have funds for research and development of new ideas and new methods, even though they may be costly to the association."

By the next year, his words would take on a new meaning as the PMA entered a time that almost destroyed it.

In early 1970, the livestock market was doing well, with stockholders making a good return for their investments. It was during this time that management of the PMA made a grave error by allowing employees to speculate on the mercantile exchange using PMA funds. Unfortunately, the market took an abrupt nose-dive, and the PMA lost $1,600,000 in only two days, wiping out the net worth of the organization. The PMA faced ruin. Fortunately, the farmers who depended on the PMA to sell their livestock were protected from direct financial loss because the organization was bonded.

Understanding how disastrous it would be if the PMA had to close its doors under these circumstances, the IFB stepped in. Two steps were needed to save it. The first was to obtain a sizable amount of capital to allow operations to continue. The second was to petition the Federal Court for an arrangement that would prevent the need to file for bankruptcy. With the cooperation of the Louisville Bank for Cooperatives, the Indiana National Bank of Indianapolis, the National Livestock Producers Association, and the IFB, Inc., both actions were taken, and the PMA continued operating.

In the early 1970s, the tax and record keeping service had a mascot called "Freddie Computer." Discussing a tax matter was Joe Edwards, right, Farm Records Service manager, and Everett Kirkendall, Clinton Co.

As IFB President George Doup wrote in *The Hoosier Farmer* at this time,

> The Farm Bureau interest at this point is to see that this cooperative livestock marketing system is saved for Indiana farmers. Without these markets throughout Indiana, farmers' income will suffer due to lack of competition. The market managers and other personnel have pledged their support and are willingly cooperating. A way out of this unfortunate situation will be found and another, stronger marketing association will be structured to serve Indiana farmers. (July 1970)

With a great deal of hard work, the marketing organization once again became financially sound. By the end of 1971, George Doup wrote in his column in *The Hoosier Farmer* that the PMA had "experienced a financial turnaround" and, if the situation continued to be positive, he expected that discussions would be held regarding ways to compensate the patiently waiting preferred stockholders.

In 1972, the PMA's new general manager, Gene Shaver, told *The Hoosier Farmer*, "We've had a good year of progress and we can point to many achievements brought about in 1971." Namely, the PMA ended fiscal year 1971 with a modest profit, substantial gains in cattle marketed, an improved cash flow, 21 markets strategically located around Indiana, and a better foundation to continue rebuilding its future. The quick action taken by the IFB had worked: In 1972, the PMA celebrated its 50th anniversary.

During that half-century, the PMA general offices were located in the Exchange Building at the Indianapolis Stockyards. Eli Lilly purchased the original stockyards property in the late 1960s and leased it to the stockyards company, but Lilly later announced that it would take possession of the property on August 15, 1973.

The new $1.5 million Indianapolis Stockyard-PMA facility was located on 16 acres on Kentucky Avenue and leased for 35 years from the Indiana Farm Bureau Cooperative Association. The PMA auction markets, country hog markets, and feeder pig receiving yards were moved to the new site, along with the general offices. The new stockyards had four acres of pens under roof, with room for 4,500 hogs, 2,000 cattle, plus after-sale pens for 3,000 hogs and 1,500 cattle. The market area under roof covered 20,000 square feet. Additional facilities included an exchange building, restaurant, bank, livestock insurance office, and animal health store. Projections called for the new market to handle $250,000,000 worth of livestock sales annually, with hogs typically going to 40 packing houses in 15 states and cattle to 30 packers in 15 states.

By the late 1960s and early 1970s, the Indiana Farm Bureau Cooperative Association had become a multi-million dollar organization working not only to provide better products for Hoosier farmers but to help them sell their products as well, even on international markets. In 1969, the total sales volume reached just over $215 million—a record figure to that time. According to the IFBCA annual report for that year, most of that volume came from grain transactions, specifically 50 million bushels of corn, 27 million bushels of soybeans, and 7 million bushels of wheat.

While this kind of sales is impressive no matter the destination of the product, it included the largest amount to that date of Hoosier grain destined for export—nearly 43 million of the total 84 million bushels. General Manager Harold P. Jordan acknowledged the role and cooperation of many facilities in this feat, including the Co-op's Gateway Elevator in Chicago, Mid-States Terminals in Toledo, the Indianapolis Terminal, and space leased at the port in Baltimore, Maryland, the departure point for Europe. (The IFBCA purchased the terminal in 1970 and spent more than $1 million to upgrade the old facility. It held four million bushels of grain.)

This international feat also required something that would have been impossible without recent improvements in transportation. During the 1969 fall harvest, 10 trains—each carrying 9,500 tons of Hoosier grain in 100 cars—made the trek from the Indianapolis Terminal to Baltimore. This was the first time the IFBCA had attempted such a feat. In addition, terminals in Chicago, Princeton, Indiana, Louisville, Indianapolis, and Toledo received 63,000 truckloads of grain, further fruits of the Indiana harvest.

Along with excellent grain sales in 1969, the IFBCA also handled cooperative marketing of other farm products, including 50 percent of the wool produced in Indiana, 500,000 turkeys, and 54 million eggs. This success, as the annual report pointed out, came about only because of the cooperation among all levels involved in the production of these products, from producers to county cooperatives. In addition, the IFBCA's improved marketing programs had been key to increasing sales. The organization pledged to continue and expand these programs in 1970, under the theme "Make More Money Through Modern Cooperative Marketing."

That slogan apparently worked, because the IFBCA, on whose board the IFB president had always served as a director-at-large, reported sales of more than $250,000,000 for 1970, thanks in part to a 23 percent increase in marketing volume from the year before. Another recent accomplishment was the successful new operation of CF Industries, Inc., a joint venture of cooperatives in 42 states and one Canadian province that included service to about 1,800,000 farmers. It was truly an example of what the IFBCA called "cooperatives unlimited."

CF Industries grew out of a desire to find a way to deliver plant food to Indiana farmers at the lowest possible cost. During the creation process, which covered several years, the IFBCA joined with other regional farmer cooperatives to acquire or build basic fertilizer production facilities. All the cooperatives involved made pledges and signed contracts guaranteeing to support those production facilities through the purchase of all their raw materials for 15 or 20 years. CF Industries built facilities to produce and deliver nitrogen, ammonia, and phosphate—the three basic raw materials of fertilizer—at costs comparable with any major American producer. In addition, it created an efficient and effective transportation, distribution, and servicing system for its products, including a 2,000-mile pipeline that carried anhydrous ammonia from Louisiana north to the Midwest. Truly, CF Industries was a reflection of "cooperatives unlimited" at its finest. This kind of joint strategy would serve farmers well as the face of agriculture continued to change.

Indiana Farm Fresh, a division of IFB's Indiana Agricultural Marketing Association, was part of a statewide network of farm markets in 1978. Rosalyn and Gene Stuckey demonstrated a "pumpkin sizer" at their market on the Boone/Hamilton County line. Prices are marked above the smallest hole that allows the pumpkin to pass through.

Chapter Two
Marketing Services And Foreign Trade

At the beginning of the 1970s, agriculture had undergone significant changes from the first days of the Farm Bureau. The business of farming had become far more complex than farmers in the 1920s could ever have imagined. No longer did more than 50 percent of the population farm; that number had fallen to around 5 percent. Small family farms were being replaced by larger farms, and farm land was increasingly being taken over by commercial and residential developments. As the cost of living continued to rise, so did the cost of farm equipment, supplies, and land—while the price farmers received for their products did not keep pace. As George Doup wrote in the January 1970 issue of *The Hoosier Farmer*,

> Capital accumulation will become a more difficult problem in the future. As agricultural enterprises grow in larger units and are fewer in number, the problem of generating capital becomes more acute.
>
> Net income in agriculture will not produce the capital needed to finance the farmer of the future. Outside capital must be attracted, but control of agriculture must not be relinquished to outside interests. Good management will help prevent this from happening.

He also emphasized that farmers must continue their group marketing strategies in responsible ways so they could match the bargaining power of the processors and merchandisers. He stated that the strategy of using the futures market to help make decisions on which crops to produce would grow in popularity since it was a way to eliminate some of the risks inherent in farming.

Another sign of upcoming changes came from the March 1970 annual meeting of the Indiana Agricultural Marketing Association. It was reported that not only farmers but the entire food industry was undergoing difficult times. IAMA Director of Marketing Robert L. Brenneman told the assembly that the number of food processors was shrinking and that those remaining were organizing into large groups, thus moving even farther from farmers. "This, in return, creates an even greater need for a strong producer's organization," he concluded.

Indiana Farm Bureau had created IAMA to assist farmers growing specific commodities. IAMA had some successes and failures, but the main strength was its programs that pulled farmers with common interests together. And it brought active farmers closer to Farm Bureau.

In the late 1960s, Paul Norris, IFB staffer, was instrumental in getting IAMA off and running. According to Brenneman, "He deserves a lot of the credit for putting together our tomato marketing program."

One successful Producers Marketing Association branch market in the 1970s was Centerville. It exhibited growth in all species marketed-cattle, hogs and sheep. Veteran employee and manager was Larry Mabe.

Brenneman pointed out that IAMA was part of American Farm Bureau's national effort to increase prices that farmers received. "We would have national and regional meetings to set goals. Primary states were Indiana, California, Ohio, New Jersey, and Illinois. We worked together on many bargaining positions and strategies."

He continued, "We had some successes with tomato bargaining in the 1970s, and growers pretty much stuck together. Through some intense bargaining we saw prices increase from $32 a ton to $65. This would not have happened without IAMA's influence."

Bargaining involved "big hitters" such as Libby Foods, Stokely VanCamp, Naas Foods, Morgan Packing Co., and Pro Fac at Mt. Summit.

"Our bargaining committee never rejected contracts with all processors in any one year. The better contracts were accepted. Others were deemed unacceptable with different companies over three or four years," Brenneman recalled.

It could be risky if IAMA growers did not approve a contract. It meant some of the growers might lose money that year. "The core producer group stuck together in most years. And all member growers made it (dollars) back the next year and then some when producers and processors signed a workable contract," Brenneman said.

IAMA, in later years, witnessed farmer complacency and contentment with contracts. Coupled with tomato harvest mechanization, a less than ideal bargaining position was being created. By the late 1970s, most of the tomato production moved to California.

IAMA tried to organize popcorn growers and was not very successful. Growers were too independent since it was easy to switch from field corn to popcorn. At that time (1970s), it was just another option. IAMA wanted Iowa involved in popcorn negotiations. Indiana and Iowa produced some 85 percent of all popcorn back then. But for various reasons Iowa Farm Bureau declined.

One AFBF program in Indiana that proved challenging was finding buyers for "spent hens." These were layers past peak egg production that were destined for processed products such as soups. "We tried to entice Hoosier producers into the program, but farmers seemed content with current processor contracts," he commented.

Following Brenneman's retirement in 1981, a fellow-employee in the Commodity Department, former fieldman and past Vanderburgh County FB President Ross Riggs assumed the role of IAMA general manger.

Riggs, who retired in 1993, pointed out that once IAMA achieved tomato contracts of $65, producers voted to disband their IAMA membership because they felt good about the current prices. "Producers were happy, and they didn't want to pay IAMA's marketing fees. As a result, prices never went much beyond that level," Riggs said. "Of course it was a disappointment to see farmers unwilling to support their marketing arm during good times but any 'fee based' system has risks from the start."

The Farm Fresh Market division was very successful from its inception in the mid-1970s. It worked with Indiana's division of agriculture on several projects as well as with the Purdue horticulture department and the Indiana Horticultural Society. IAMA members were listed in the state's farm market brochure.

IAMA's Farm Fresh (roadside market program) member-map brochure was a success. "The entire program was a good one. Our members maintained high quality and abided by certain guidelines. We gave the consumer a Hoosier-grown product of tremendously high quality," Riggs emphasized.

"In those days our board of directors felt that IAMA and its affiliates should be showing a profit. Once joining IAMA, most of our services were free. The irony was that at the same time Commodity and other departments were providing many services to help agriculture free of charge," Riggs mentioned.

IAMA was responsible for marketing Purdue Swiss-type cheese. "For a number of years," Riggs went on, "the profits from this program contributed significant dollars to the scholarship programs of Purdue Ag Alumni Association."

Another popular seller in the 1970s was Wisconsin cheese. In many instances, primarily processed cheeses were available to members at grocery stores. "We made mild and sharp cheddar available and later added caraway. One order figure I remember was 23,000 pounds of cheese that we sold along with citrus in the county offices," Riggs said.

In 1969 IAMA began talks with Florida Farm Bureau. "I remember in 1970 we brought 17 semi-trailer loads of oranges and grapefruit to IFB members, " Riggs remembered. Over the years Florida reciprocated and helped market Indiana popcorn. The citrus program ended in 1994.

Brenneman and Riggs both agreed, "Our marketing programs were member-driven, and we were Farm Bureau and everyone knew it. During the last years of IAMA, you had to be a member in order the benefit from IAMA and

IFB's movie, "Food...From Farm to You" was presented to John Loughlin, State Superintendent of Public Instruction. Movie copies were made available statewide for showing in schools. (l. to r.) Glenn W. Sample, IFB vice president; Loughlin; Becky Surface and C. W. Stall, Information & Public Relations Department.

IFB President George Doup, seated, accepted a symbolic check from Don Henderson, IFB Organization Department, representing 1972 membership attainment. With nine consecutive years of growth, membership totaled 207,326. The figure represented an all-time high in Indiana's history.

Farm Fresh. And it was good for Farm Bureau to be able to represent such an important segment of agriculture.

"We were able to establish relationships to help individual producers and increase their chances to make more money. We were a valuable resource and helped producer-members in many ways. And a lot of those members are still active."

The challenges faced by Indiana farmers in the 1970s had changed from those they faced 50 years earlier. However, the attitude and work ethic of the IFB had not. Doup was optimistic that the 1970s would be a good decade for Indiana farmers. He declared, "Farmers and Farm Bureau must face the future with desire and determination. It will pay dividends."

Among the new challenges were changes in production and marketing. The Indiana Agricultural Marketing Association had been created a decade earlier, in large part to help Hoosier tomato farmers deal with just these changes by increasing their bargaining power. By the early 1970s, the IAMA could say that all contracts they negotiated on behalf of tomato growers resulted in more net income to the growers, sometimes up to 40 to 50 percent a ton. Among the contract improvements the IAMA had instituted were improved delivery schedules, improved hauling and dumping methods, improved seeds and plants, and designations of grade types.

While the IAMA stated that stronger bargaining and marketing were crucial to farmers, the organization also supported the Marketing and Bargaining Act of 1971, also known as the Sisk bill. This collective bargaining bill for farmers would require processors and producers associations to bargain in good faith. The IFB concurred.

This bill was written at the Farm Bureau's insistence and with its support. Members believed this kind of bill was necessary because contract marketing terms had traditionally been developed by handlers and offered to producers on a one-sided, take-it-or-leave it basis.

The bill would remedy this situation with its two main provisions. First, it would establish a three-member National Agricultural Bargaining Board to determine "qualified" bargaining associations. The second provision would establish the mutual obligation of handlers and a qualified association to deal in good faith in all aspects of their transactions regarding contract marketing.

The bill originally had good support in Congress when it came up for hearings in late 1971. The most intense opposition came, not unexpectedly, from processors and handlers, who were unwilling to give up the advantages they had in the bargaining process. The next year, Congress failed to pass the bill. The Farm Bureau warned that not passing the Sisk bill would risk greater problems in the future, including the imposition of compulsory bargaining and highly restrictive supply management restrictions.

The early 1970s were marked by another challenge to farmers, one that demonstrated how closely various sectors of the economy in the United States and other countries had to work together for farmers to succeed. During the summer of 1971, longshoremen at Chicago ports and on the East and West coasts went on strike at harvest time, refusing to load ships bound for foreign ports. For the months of July and August alone, an estimated $215 million worth of farm products was not shipped; $40 million worth of perishable fruits and vegetables were ruined, and grains piled up in elevators and spoiled on the ground. The losses eventually mounted into the billions of dollars.

The Farm Bureau called for government intervention, asking that legislation be passed to prevent such situations in the future. The Taft Hartley Act was invoked to get the longshoremen back to work for a cooling off period, yet the West Coast longshoremen resumed their strike several months later, which dragged on into the spring of 1972. Secretary of Agriculture Earl Butz, a native of Indiana, supported the farmers in their pleas, and Congress passed a temporary measure to order the West Coast union back to work. George Doup and the IFB called for a permanent law regarding transportation disputes such as the dock workers' strike that would allow an injunction to be issued to force strikers back to work.

Hollys Moon, IFB Legislative Department, helped a fair visitor select a free Farm Bureau pencil in the Farmer's Building during the Indiana State Fair in 1972.

The Rural Youth Singers, comprised of members throughout Indiana, performed at the 1972 Indiana State Fair. Their singing was a tradition for many years.

Warren Wheaton (left) IFB District 9 director, welcomes AFBF President William J. Kuhfuss (center) to their 1972 district meeting. Insurance personnel also attended along with George Doup (right) IFB president.

In 1972, dock strikes loomed again. Maritime unions around the country threatened to refuse to load grain on foreign ships, saying that more American ships had to be used for shipment to protect the livelihoods of their members. Such a move would have destroyed the new billion dollar grain sale to the Soviet Union. Grain companies fought back by filing or threatening to file injunctions to force the longshoremen and other unions sympathetic to their cause to go back to work. The IFB and other state Farm Bureaus once again called for federal legislation to prevent these strikes in the future. With one-fourth of U. S. agricultural products now being shipped overseas and American farmers depending on those international sales, *The Hoosier Farmer* declared, "If the U.S. export market is to be maintained or expanded, foreign purchasers must have assurance that we will be able to deliver our goods anywhere and on schedule, otherwise they will fill their orders elsewhere." (November 1972). Congress did not take action, yet the existing maritime union situation resolved itself.

In 1972, $10 billion worth of U. S. agricultural products were exported, a 25 percent increase in farm exports in one year. In the first three months of 1973, export sales had jumped to $3.7 billion, or 73 percent above the same period one year earlier. (More than $384 million of those exports came from Indiana, primarily in feed grains, soybeans, and dairy products.) The countries that imported the largest amounts of American farm products were the Soviet Union, China, Japan, and West Germany.

This leap in the amount of exports was hailed as the beginning of a new era in American agriculture, one in which farmers could export more of their products around the world and then they would be less dependent on the government for their income. Even so, farmers would have continuing challenges—many would call them crises—throughout the decade.

The 1970s was the time when concern about environmental problems began to surface and grow across the United States. Congress established the Environmental Protection Agency in 1970 to oversee environmental legislation and its enforcement. While the IFB agreed with the agency in principle, it was concerned about how the agency would compose and enforce new legislation and what effect it would have on farmers.

One area that occasioned an editorial in *The Hoosier Farmer* was the transfer of pesticide regulation from the U.S. Department of Agriculture to the new EPA. The USDA understood the importance of pesticides in modern farming, and the IFB was not confident the EPA would have the same understanding. An editorial by C. W. Stall, editor, stated,

> Should supervision (of pesticide regulation) fall under the control of what could easily be an over-emotional and non-understanding government agency, the impact on the business of farming and

In 1972, Gubernatorial candidates Otis Bowen (top photo) and Matthew Welsh (bottom photo) visited with George Doup, IFB president, prior to talking with county presidents in Indianapolis. Both candidates stressed the importance of agriculture maintaining a strong voice in the Hoosier state.

on the pocketbook of urban consumers could be disastrous. . . Farmers see no reasons to change horses in the middle of a winning race. (August 1970)

During the ensuing years, *The Hoosier Farmer* kept its readers up-to-date on the latest environmental regulations as they affected farmers. One set of regulations covered effluent discharge standards to be applied to some livestock feedlots, dairy facilities, and poultry installations. The proposed requirement of zero discharge was deemed "unreasonable" by the IFB, which claimed that some farmers would be forced out of business or be forced to quit feeding or milking because of the too-high cost of meeting the requirements. Farmers were willing to control run-off to protect water sources, but the IFB asked that local weather conditions be taken into account in determining the discharge standards.

In early 1973, the EPA announced its intention to cancel registration of chemicals containing Aldrin and Dieldrin, two soil insecticides widely used by farmers. George Doup included a few remarks about this decision in his address to the 1973 IFB convention:

> Farmers are not major polluters of the land, water, air or environment. Farmers will willingly comply with reasonable and realistic restrictions. But emotion-oriented, factually-unfounded regulations and orders have no place in agriculture. Consumers will see food costs rise rapidly if unnecessary and unjustified production cost-increasing factors are imposed on farmers.

Acord Cantwell, director of the IFB Natural Resources Department, later wrote in *The Hoosier Farmer* that "there is a real danger that politicians and public manipulation of our aspiration to accomplish a clean environment will destroy the very productivity we need to achieve it" (May 1973). He stated that a concern for ecology must be balanced with concern for the economy. This has been a constant refrain of the IFB ever since the 1970s, as the amount and severity of environmental regulation has continued to escalate—often, in the eyes of the Farm Bureau, at farmers' expense.

Many farmers in the early 1970s felt they simply moved from one crisis to the next during those years. Transportation, a crucial link in the agricultural economy, presented them with a major crisis at that time. For many years, railroads had played a major role in U. S. and Indiana agriculture. The vast network of tracks crisscrossing the country gave farmers access to many markets, even international ones, that they otherwise would not have been able to reach. But for six major railroads in the Northeast, including the gigantic Penn-Central, bankruptcy loomed—a situation that could easily throw agriculture and many other sectors of the economy into peril. As *The Hoosier Farmer* of

September 1973 stated, "Trucks, planes and boats serve well in their place, but they simply can't do the job when it comes to moving bulky, heavy loads, like machinery, grain, coal, lumber, fertilizer, and hundreds of other items." Hoosier farmers produced the sixth-highest volume of farm products exported and so depended on railroads to carry, in 1973 alone, $384 million in feed grains, soybeans and soybean oil, oil and cake meals, and dairy products to ports for export.

Therefore, Farm Bureau called on Congress to take emergency action to keep the railroads running, short of a government take-over. Congress did take action, passing the Railway Reorganization Act. It aimed to restructure the surviving rail system in the Northeast portion of the country, which included Indiana.

Another aspect of transportation grabbed national attention about this same time. An oil embargo by the Arab countries—the Organization of Petroleum Exporting Countries, or OPEC—that produced much of the world's supply caused a drastic reduction of petroleum products in the United States. Almost overnight, the price of oil skyrocketed 400 percent as supplies dropped precipitously. This situation came to be known as the energy crisis. It was primarily depicted through photos of long lines of vehicles waiting at gas stations and by a sweater-wearing President Jimmy Carter who asked the nation to lower its thermostats in an effort to conserve energy.

Farmers were hard hit, since they required large amounts of fuel not only to get their products to market but also to operate their large field machinery and to dry certain crops. The Indiana Farm Bureau composed a resolution which, according to *The Hoosier Farmer*, "asks that continuing priority be given these needs in the production, harvesting and drying of farm products. It also urges all farmers to assume responsibility for conserving energy wherever possible." *The Indianapolis News* praised this resolution as sound policy.

Harold Jordan, IFBCA general manager, pledged that "no farmer would go without fuel" during that crop year. Therefore, using its refinery, pipeline systems, and truck transport network, the IFBCA did its part during the 1973 energy crisis by delivering 23 percent more gasoline and 46 percent more diesel fuel to its farmer customers than it did the year before. The co-op refinery at Mt. Vernon ran at capacity for many months to accomplish this feat, using crude oil from the Illinois basin and from government-royalty crude from offshore Louisiana sources.

The federal government had decreed that farmers should receive the highest priority call for fuel for the duration of the energy crisis, and the general public agreed. Therefore, the IFB urged Hoosier farmers to remember that this priority referred only to farm production. Declared *The Hoosier Farmer*, "If it appears that farmers are wasting gasoline, diesel fuel or gas or using it unduly

California Governor Ronald Reagan, was keynote speaker at the 54th annual AFBF convention in Los Angeles, December 10-14, 1972. The evening entertainment was Lawrence Welk and his orchestra.

for pleasure driving, public opinion can turn negative overnight, and food producers will lose face as well as fuel. This, agriculture cannot afford to have happen." The IFB urged local leaders around the state to combine meetings to reduce unnecessary driving, and the board of directors took the lead by combining three large district meetings into one. Even the IFBCA instructed its employees to fuel their company cars elsewhere. As *The Hoosier Farmer* warned, "...farmers must accept the fact that they are under the microscope of public opinion right now, and they must give their best performance in conservation and food production."

The energy crisis continued into 1977 and 1978, leading to more government intervention to help solve the problem. However, the IFB believed that many government actions in this regard were inadequate. An October 1977 editorial in *The Hoosier Farmer* stated,

> The Administration in Washington and the Congress seem to be doing little to find a lasting solution to the energy crisis facing us all. The program being pushed there is based on conservation alone, and little or no incentive is given to oil and gas companies to find and develop new and larger supplies...
>
> The "no-program" energy program seems designed to drive oil and gas users back to coal; yet it is rumored that coal miners are just waiting for cooler weather to pull off a big coal strike.
>
> Farmers must have adequate energy available to produce food, or we could get hungry in a hurry. Farmers believe that we should conserve energy, but we should get on with development of new sources for the future when we will no doubt require far more energy than is now necessary. By discouraging incentives our national leaders are endangering our security and lowering our standard of living.

All the problems that afflicted Hoosier farmers in the early and mid-1970s were set against a larger backdrop of high inflation combined with threatened and actual government intervention in the business of growing food. From foreign grain embargoes to the proposed establishment of a world food reserve, these actions were seen by farmers as counterproductive to their interests.

Early in the decade, the government called for increased farm production to make up for shortfalls caused by poor weather and other causes. It seemed that all-out production was justified, since market prices were good, the amount of food reserves was down, and domestic and foreign demand was high. Yet at the same time, high inflation caused the government to impose price ceilings on some agricultural products, such as beef, in response to consumer demands to keep prices low. While even the IFB said a ceiling on beef prices was not terribly damaging, the organization decried it as having a negative affect on farm production. As George Doup said in his September 1973 editorial, farmers "are not going to feed chickens, raise hogs, produce beef or grow canning crops at a time when the prospect of a profit is practically nil."

He continued,

> We have the agricultural capacity in this country to feed our people well and to fill much of the deficient food and feed grain needs of people in many of the other countries. There will be times in the short run when weather, economic conditions or other factors cause some unusual production and price maladjustments. Given time and satisfactory prices, farmers will correct such situations. Controls will not. (September 1973)

A major part of the problem was that the general public saw and read many accounts regarding rising food prices, but they were not nearly as well informed about the farmer's plight when prices dropped. "Politicians and consumers must understand that the low food prices of the past are not possible with the increased costs of production incurred by farmers today," said George Doup. "The clock can't be turned back." He called for the news media to tell the "whole and accurate story" of agricultural economics.

Another factor in the 1970s agricultural equation was the new high levels of agricultural exports. They reached nearly $13 billion in fiscal year 1973, with the Soviet Union alone purchasing $1.2 billion worth of wheat, corn, and soybeans that year. Even so, some in Congress wanted to impose embargoes on these sales, holding down the amount of grain and other U. S. farm products that could be sold overseas. Since one-quarter of all farm products were now sold to foreign countries, halting or reducing the amount of exports would serve to depress the U. S. and Indiana farm economy. The IFB called for increases in agricultural exports, not decreases. Secretary of Agriculture Earl Butz supported the Farm Bureau's position to let the market system function without intervention, but he seemed to be a lone voice in government. However, in October 1974, in an event that came to be known in agricultural circles as "Black Friday," President Nixon cancelled the sale of 1 million tons of corn and 2.4 million tons of wheat to the Soviet Union. This action caused chaos in the international grain market and hit Indiana farmers very hard in a year when a wet planting season, a summer drought, and an early freeze had already devastated their crops.

After this incident, the presidents of several state Farm Bureaus, including George Doup, urged Secretary Butz and the President to end the export restrictions, such as monitoring and embargoes, on farm exports. They insisted that farmers, before planting time, must have "concrete assurance" from the government that embargoes will not be applied during the following year.

Late in 1974, Congress passed the Trade Reform Act of 1974. The IFB commended them for passing the bill, which was the first important trade legislation passed since the Kennedy administration in 1962. The new act gave the President the power to conduct actions that would help open new trade doors around the world. The act emphasized an increase in trade to less-developed countries, which would help them decrease their dependence on financial aid.

Even so, occasional resistance to selling farm products overseas still erupted in the private sector. In one instance, grain sales to the Soviet Union were held up as a protest over Russian restrictions on Jewish emigration. (In fact, this incident almost prevented passage of the Trade Reform Act of 1974. The IFB held that it should have been dealt with diplomatically, rather than as a trade issue.)

In the fall of 1975, again at harvest time, farmers were prevented from sending some of their products overseas when George Meany, president of the AFL-CIO, called a strike of the Longshoremen's Union. This action was a drastic turn-around in the position of organized labor, which for many years had supported free trade. Union members refused to load wheat on ships bound for the Soviet Union. The publicized reason behind the strike was ostensibly to keep food prices down in this time of 7 to 10 percent inflation, although the Farm Bureau blasted Meany for holding farmers hostage to the economy in this way. Other reasons behind the strike, said the union, was job protection and higher wages for union members.

Even though Indiana wheat was not involved, George Doup and the IFB protested the action. Doup sent a letter to President Gerald Ford asking him and Congress and the courts to prevent "such irresponsible actions" on the part of labor. He also sent a letter to George Meany, reprinted in *The Hoosier Farmer*, which read, in part,

> Denying farmers access to much needed foreign markets as a means to satisfy some of the selfish desires of labor is unwarranted and un-American. And to try to justify such actions by posing to be the grand champion of the food consumer is irresponsible and thinly veiled...
> Prices to farmers are not excessive. To force the holding of grains in this country as a means of lowering food prices places all the economic impact of such actions on the backs of farmers. This is unjustified and is a harsh pill for farmers to swallow. If food prices go higher, it will be for other reasons than the market prices farmers are now receiving.

The IFB believed in unrestricted foreign trade for farm products, saying it was essential for the national economy. For one group like the labor unions to take an action that curtailed exports of farm products hurt the entire economy, not just farmers. Unfortunately, the Administration's first response to the strike was to place an embargo on sales of grain to the Soviet Union. Then, the State Department negotiated an agreement that locked in an annual Soviet purchase of 6 million metric tons of wheat and feed grains for five years. It also allowed the sale of an additional 2 million tons to be sold to them without prior government approval, unless U. S. grain stocks fell below 225 million tons. Any purchase over this 8 million tons required the approval of both governments.

The IFB was incensed that the State Department, rather than Agriculture, handled the agreement. In his 1976 address to the IFB convention, after noting that grain prices broke once the agreement was announced, Doup said, "This agreement sets a dangerous precedent and is a damaging departure from allowing farmers free market access. Limiting markets hurts market prices." He worried that Congress would eventually be granted the right to control agricultural export sales, leaving the country's farmers at the mercy of "cheap food advocates" who worked to keep prices low at the very literal expense of farmers. As he said, "Farmers cannot tolerate government's pleading for all-out crop production, at planting time, and then depriving farmers, at harvest time, of access to markets...(This) is just a clever ruse to hold down food prices and farmers can see through this quite readily."

At the same time that the nation demanded lower food prices, farmers were receiving less of each food dollar than previously. During the decade prior to 1974, food prices rose steadily while the farm value of food items and the retail value widened at a greater rate. A 1974 study by the American Farm Bureau Federation found that farmers were receiving 4 percent less than they had in 1973, which was the highest percent in 18 years. The biggest costs in the food marketing bill were labor, packaging, and transportation, in that order. Said *The Hoosier Farmer*,

> While almost all costs have been increased by inflationary trends of recent years...the fact remains that labor has been able to increase substantially its share of the total food marketing bill through its ability to demand and receive higher wages. Government labor-management relations policies and government monetary and fiscal policies have strengthened labor's hand in this regard. (August 1974)

Finally, in early 1976, the dock workers strike was settled with the intervention of the National Labor Relations Board. The maritime unions involved agreed to cease and desist from engaging in similar work stoppages in the future. *The Hoosier Farmer* reported the motive of the union was not concern for food prices, but rather "an insistence on a maritime cargo preference agreement with increased maritime subsidies to be paid by American taxpayers," with farmers being used as political pawns.

The IFB had a strong governmental ally in the person of Secretary of Agriculture Earl Butz. A native of Noble County, Indiana, he believed, as did

Indiana Governor Otis Bowen, seated, announced May 24, 1976, that Indiana Farm Bureau and the Indiana State Fair board had signed an agreement for air conditioning the auditorium and exhibit hall of the newly named Farm Bureau Building, formerly the Farmers Building at the State Fair. Discussing the announcement are from left: George Doup, IFB president; Estel Callahan, ISF secretary/manager; Dwight Smoker, 1976 fair board president, and C. W. Stall, IFB Information & Public Relations Department.

the IFB, that the best way to deal with excess agricultural capacity was through a "vigorous and growing export market," as he told those in attendance at the 1973 IFB convention. He said that the alternate strategy of curtailing farm production, or "government-created scarcity," did not work, as was evidenced by 40 years of such policies.

Butz favored open trade for agricultural products, rather than administered trade, under which governments established trade and production patterns through international agreements. He concluded his talk by saying, "Only open trade will give American agriculture the opportunity it seeks and the American economy the stimulation it needs."

Despite the dwindling number of people involved in farming from earlier in the century, agriculture still played a large role in the national economy Butz referred to. That was also true of the Indiana economy. A Purdue study done in the mid-1970s revealed a great deal of the value of the state's agricultural pursuits. For instance, there were 106,000 farms, with an average size of 165 acres. About 76 percent of the state's land, or 17.5 million acres, was devoted to agriculture, with 85 of the 92 counties having more than half their land in use as farms. With the average per-acre land value of the time, this meant that Indiana agricultural producers had over $138 billion, or an average of $140,000 per farm, invested in their land and buildings. All this land was worked by about 126,000 farm operators and their family members, or about 2.25 percent of all Hoosiers.

Indiana ranked high among the 50 states in the production of various food products: third in soybeans and hog production, fifth in corn and tomatoes, seventh in eggs, eighth in turkeys, ninth in all crops and in all agricultural production, and twelfth in all livestock.

One statistic demonstrated in a direct way how greatly farmers contributed to the overall state economy. Every increase of $1,000 in agricultural production caused an additional $2,634 increase in economic activity. This figure broke down into $738 for manufacturing, $1,080 for the trade and service sectors, and $816 in additional household income.

Each farm worker was matched by two workers in manufacturing, trade, and services needed to furnish farms with materials required to produce, process, deliver, and sell their products. Each $1 million of Hoosier farm production created employment for about 98 non-farm workers.

Additionally, $115 million in Indiana property taxes in 1974 came from farmers. This amounted to 12 percent of the total property taxes collected—from only about 2.4 percent of the population.

With these figures to back them up, farmers could easily demonstrate to nonbelievers the positive effect their work had on the economy of the state.

Unfortunately, the federal government at times seemed unable to grasp the significance of the agricultural portion of the economy to the nation's total economy. For instance, in addition to trying to limit foreign trade as a way of affecting food prices, the federal government also established giant grain reserves during times of over-production as a hedge against leaner times. The IFB did not appreciate this meddling with the market, believing that the open market was better for farmers and consumers alike.

An international World Food Conference held in Rome in the mid-1970s called for huge world food reserves to be established to help less-developed countries that could not produce enough food. The American Farm Bureau Federation believed this policy would be not only costly and wasteful but harmful to the developing countries, since it would do nothing to encourage them to improve food production. The AFBF, with strong support from Secretary of Agriculture Butz, instead supported a monetary reserve from which countries in need of food could receive loans or grants so they could purchase food from the more affluent countries, which would contribute to the fund.

George Doup called government-controlled grain reserves "subtle but devastating ways of holding down prices" to the detriment of the farmer. Any benefits derived from the reserves would be short-lived, he said, since farmers "cannot be expected to produce when the cards are stacked against their making a profit." An editorial in *The Hoosier Farmer* declared,

> It is no more logical to have a national or world food reserve in the hands of the U. S government than it is to have a national gasoline bank, coal bank, automobile bank, or clothing reserve. Who says the government can store the food reserves of this country better than farmers and the food processing industry? Those who do, want it that way so they can control it. (June 1974)

During the early 1970s, when inflation had caused food prices to rise quite a bit, sentiment for the grain reserves was high among the general public, who believed that the use of the reserved grain would help keep prices down. Another common belief, which the IFB held to be false, was that the food supply would be jeopardized without massive government-controlled reserves. The IFB sought to educate the public, as well as government officials, about the fallacies of these arguments and the real cost of the reserves.

Furthermore, government farm policies did not always produce the hoped-for results. For instance, during earlier years when huge grain reserves were put on the market, prices sometimes went up, not down. Also, it was often true that farmers did much better financially when the government was less actively involved in farm programs. From 1973-1976, for example, farmers had the highest realized net income in the previous 40 years, a nationwide total of about $25 billion. This came during a time when they had the least amount of "help" from farm programs than any time during that 40 years. *The Hoosier Farmer* declared, "We told you so."

The magazine also declared that, in coming years, the most important factor in reaching growing production goals would be the political climate in which farmers would be producing. An editorial by C. W. Stall in May 1976 declared,

> If regulatory restrictions, government program discouragements, market-killing political activities, and other bureaucratic controls are allowed to continue to grow, farmers will not be lured by the opportunity for profit, and food goals will not be reached.
> Farmers will feed our people well if given the freedom, the opportunity and the financial incentive to do so. This truth has been proved here in the U. S., and in many foreign countries. This is no time to choose political leaders who would tighten the government-control noose around the farmers' necks.

Urban growth, water issues, taxes, and a declining farmer population continue to challenge the very fabric of agriculture.

Chapter Three
Patterns Of Change

As if farmers did not have enough problems to deal with in the 1970s, the decade brought into sharp focus the larger picture of a society undergoing transformation, changing so quickly and so drastically that farming in the United States and in Indiana would never return to the same patterns it had maintained for generations.

By the mid-20th century, the number of farms in the United States and Indiana had begun to decline, sometimes rapidly. The reasons for this were many. As farming methods improved, fewer farmers were needed to produce the same—or larger—amounts of food. Rising costs combined with lower prices for their products forced out many farmers who could no longer afford to keep their expensive operations going, especially in times of high inflation and extended bad weather, like the 1970s and 1980s. Growing cities and suburbs expanded into surrounding areas that had previously been farmland. In times of rising property taxes, farmers sometimes had to sell off parcels of land to pay taxes on their remaining property, a situation about which *The Hoosier Farmer* said, "This means the breakup of prime farm operating units in order to pay taxes on land assessed at rates no farm enterprise can afford to pay." More and more farmers had to work off the farm to supplement their agricultural income. By 1969, nearly two-thirds of Indiana farmers, often the women in the family, were working off the farm 100 or more days a year.

When the IFB formed in 1919, 50 percent of the population was directly involved in farming. By the 1960s and early 1970s, the number was closer to 5 percent, and still declining. The IFB, always responsive to the needs of its members, kept a close eye on the changing situation. In several issues in the early 1970s, *The Hoosier Farmer* reported on the farm decline.

One article reported on the encroachment of urban areas into prime farmland:

> Farmland is becoming scarce. North America's expanding population, expected to increase by more than 76 million people by 1991, coupled with deteriorating cities, new highway systems and an ever-growing horde of automobiles, is responsible for pushing new homes, businesses and factories out of urban areas. And as they move to the suburbs, fertile land is being displaced at an alarming rate. (February 1972)

By that time, 1 million acres of United States farmland were being taken out of production every year. Indiana was not immune from this trend. The number of Hoosier farms declined 16 percent from 1959 to 1964; in the next five years, the rate slowed to only 6 percent. Since that time, the numbers have continued their downward slide. However, as the total number of farms declined, the size of the remaining farms increased. From 1964 to 1969, the size of the remaining Indiana farms increased by a total of seven acres. This was another trend that would continue, as farms required more acreage to support increased costs and as mechanization made this kind of growth possible.

As *The Hoosier Farmer* reported, in the early 1970s most of the farms in the country and in Indiana were still owned by families and individuals, although the number of corporate-owned farms was growing. Many farms, both family- and corporate-owned, were becoming quite large, a fact that seemed to alarm some bankers and agribusinessmen. George Doup cited a report from the Federal Reserve Bank of Kansas City that said, "Agricultural production increasingly is shifting into the hands of large commercial operations," the implication being that this was a negative development, a conclusion with which Doup and the IFB disagreed.

Doup speculated on what could have generated this report and a spate of others similar to it:

> We wonder if some agribusinessmen are afraid that farmers might be close to putting it all together—efficient production, controlled marketing, just pricing, etc.—and starting to get their fair share of the country's prosperity. . .

There are many agribusinessmen who like government support programs for farm commodities, even though such programs stymie incentive and keep farm prices at a poverty level. . .

There are some who enjoy extra security or profit by letting the farmer take the risk or, through government storage programs, let the taxpayers carry their raw material inventories and hold farm prices down. Included are millers, meat packers, canners, and a number of other food processors and distributors.

We hope the mixed outpouring of "concern" for the consumer and the farmer is an indication that farmers are beginning to impress those in the agribusiness world with the importance of food production, with their trend toward cooperative marketing, and with the importance of food as a pawn in world finance and politics. (*The Hoosier Farmer*, August 1974)

He reminded farmers that they still had a powerful voice, that they still had political clout, but that they would not be heard unless they continued to participate in the political process and took action on those issues that concerned them.

The first Youth Safety Seminar was held in 1973 in Bainbridge. YOUSAFE was designed for high school freshmen and sophomores. Classes included defensive driving, first aid, firearms, tractor & equipment, electrical, water, and home & babysitting during this 1976 session.

Beginning in the 1970s, the IFB began calling for more effective community land use decisions, particularly in urban fringes encroaching upon farmland:

> Even though there is probably no perfect or absolute solution to the problem of proper land-use, it seems that a combination of zoning, developed through the use of up-to-date soil surveys, is the most viable answer. And cooperative coordination is the key. Farmers and non-farm persons must work together to solve such mutual problems as roadside erosion control, flooding and silting, locating proper recreation sites, highway planning, sewage disposal and location of housing and industrial developments. Through effective use of the land-planning tools available today, progress may be measured in terms of what is best economically and ecologically. (February 1972).

In the early 1970s, public pressure was developing for legislation that would remove from land owners any control over how their land was to be developed and used. The EPA issued a report that commented that states and localities alone cannot always be expected to make the most appropriate land use choices. These smaller bodies, according to the report, were not able to assess and determine national goals and perspective, which is something the EPA believed was important in land use policies.

George Doup called the report "gobbledegook" and derided the EPA view that local and regional residents couldn't make the right decisions but national bureaucrats could. He said the report "makes clear that there are those in high places in government who want the authority to tell you and me the exact use we may make of our farms." He said a middle path must be found, where farmers must not be unduly restricted or hurt and where the public interest will be recognized.

In September 1973, the IFB sponsored a Land-Use Planning Conference to put current Indiana land use in perspective and to review proposed federal legislation on the subject. More than 450 representatives from business, industry, government, and agriculture attended. They agreed that competition for land would continue to intensify and that planning would grow increasingly important. In addition, they agreed that land-use planning should not be handled at the state level and certainly not at the federal level, but at the local level. *The Hoosier Farmer* warned that farmers attending the conference "should have gotten the message that they must become more interested in land use plans, and become much more active than they have ever been in developing plans to make them practical and workable."

One provision in a federal bill worried the IFB. The provision called for sanctions against states, such as the withholding of grants, as a way of coercing states to adopt certain land use policies. The Senate killed this particular provision, but Doup warned that "its ugly head, however, will rise again and again."

To back up its contention that land use be decided at the local level, the IFB included a section on land use planning in its 1974 policy statement. The IFB called for voluntary land-use authorities formed for specific time periods and which favored agriculture as the highest priority use. It recommended that government-employed representatives should serve only in advisory capacities on regional and state planning bodies. It also recommended that county farm bureaus be actively involved in land use planning and zoning in their communities to protect farmers and their interests.

In June 1974, the U.S. House of Representatives killed the bill, H. R. 10294 - Land Use Planning Act of 1973, from which the sanctions provision had been eliminated. The IFB cheered the death of the dangerous bill.

New government regulation intruded into the long-established Cooperative Extension Service in the early 1970s, to the dismay of the Extension Service itself and Indiana farmers. For nearly 75 years, the Extension Service had provided adult education for farmers and assisted organizations like 4-H Clubs and Home Demonstration clubs. From the beginning, it was open to all citizens. In the 1970s, the notion of mandated equal opportunity became part of government regulation, and the Extension Service was reorganized to ensure its availability to everyone who wanted to participate.

In 1974, IFB Organization Department's field staff included: (l. to r.) Front row: Charles Dow, Gary Moore, Mike Jones, Jerry Couch, and Dick Lowe. Middle row: Wilmer Burrous, Bob Jenkins, Jim York, Gene Pflug, Hayden King, and Marvin Metzger. Back row: Don Henderson, department head; Harry Pearson, Bob Downin, Oren Chumley, and Frank Larsen.

The original plan of the Extension Service called for each county to have one or more agents who were responsible for their counties. This system had worked well, according to Hoosier farmers, for nearly three-quarters of a century. Under the new system, the state was divided into "areas," and agents, who had been able to deal with all aspects of Extension Service programs, were required to become specialists in one of more than a dozen areas of expertise. These specialists had to serve more than one county. This organization proved inconvenient and confusing for farmers, because it was now difficult to know whom to contact for what information.

Complying with new equal opportunity regulations also bogged down the Extension Service with additional paperwork, which lessened the time available for programs and working with farmers. *The Hoosier Farmer* carried an editorial in December 1972 that explained the IFB position on these new regulations:

> ...now that "equal opportunity" is receiving priority attention; the words advertised on Extension correspondence; and all sorts of time-consuming records kept just to prove that there is not discrimination, many former enthusiasts feel that their Extension workers are so bogged down with ridiculous busywork that they hesitate to get involved, let alone "bleed and die" for local and state appropriations.
>
> It is clear that if the Cooperative Extension Service makes a determined effort to do all that they are supposed to with their present, voluntary clientele, with the disadvantaged, with the low income, with ALL youth, and with ALL adults, and keep all of the records necessary to prove that they are doing it, vast additional revenue and vast expansion of staff are going to be needed.

Purdue University, under whose authority and guidance the Cooperative Extension Service operated in Indiana, worked to streamline the new system and keep the service easily accessible to its clients while complying with the new regulations. Because the power of the Extension Service came from its service to farmers, farmers had to remain the major focus. A study committee that worked for many months developed a plan called "Operation Future." Based on the plan, the Extension Service made several positive changes in its organization; program, staffing, and training policies; reporting; and inter-program communication. It improved local coordination of programs and gave local offices more responsibility for program planning and resource procurement. State program leaders were established in four areas: agriculture, community development, home economics, and youth. Furthermore, a state staff member was assigned to perfect a staff training and professional development program.

Purdue vowed to continue serving farmers through the Cooperative Extension Service under "Operation Future." The university's dean of agriculture, R. L. Kohls, stated at an Extension Service conference,

> We [Purdue] have decided that it will be possible to have excellence in all our agricultural functions at Purdue—the classroom teaching, the research operation, and the extension function. The problem of orientation of our clientele is the focal point regardless of whether it takes several disciplines or departments, several researchers combined with extension people, specialists on the campus or in the field, or a combination of all. (*The Hoosier Farmer*, August 1973)

By 1975, the Extension Service and the Agricultural Experiment Stations had been assigned 25 regulatory tasks in agricultural areas. Among these tasks were the supervision of purity and proper labeling of seed, feed, and fertilizer offered for sale in Indiana. The state creamery license law and the state's egg act were administered through Purdue, as well as the pesticide, ammonia, and legume inoculant laws. Purdue also handled agricultural statistics; soil testing; corn, soybean, and sorghum performance testing; and swine evaluation.

In cooperation with the U.S. Department of Agriculture, Purdue handled five inspection services; federal-state turkey improvement plans; national poultry and turkey improvement plans; fresh fruit and vegetable inspection; grading of experimental tobacco; and educational activities related to tobacco grades.

All these programs helped to protect farmers and the general public. By placing these responsibilities with Purdue, a land grant college long involved in agricultural pursuits, the federal and state governments placed the work where it could most efficiently and effectively be accomplished.

By the late 1970s, Purdue was in need of a new agricultural research facility. As IFB President Marion Stackhouse wrote in an editorial,

> The need for research is growing by leaps and bounds, and in many areas which were of little concern in past years. Some of the difficult problems of the future will be —ways of conserving energy in the food industry, as well as to find renewable energy sources; basic research in many chemical and physical aspects of our food industry as it affects the human sector; and new efficiency methods in the production of meat and grain.
>
> Governmental agencies are constantly looking to Purdue for research data to decide public policy issues. To meet these needs, additional space and new controlled research labs will be necessary for Purdue to participate in the research data bank so vitally needed by our country. (*The Hoosier Farmer*, November 1978)

Agricultural Research Center

Indiana Farm Bureau supported Purdue's efforts for a new agricultural research building. Ceremonial ground breaking took place in 1980. Wielding the shovel is Indiana Gov. Otis R. Bowen, M.D.

R. L. Kohls, Purdue dean of agriculture, called the university's Agricultural Experiment Station "a major contributor to Indiana's agricultural success story," with its agricultural scientists and educators receiving international acclaim for their accomplishments. But he also stated in the January 1979 issue of *The Hoosier Farmer* that the time had come for a new research facility.

The initial plans were approved by the Indiana Commission on Higher Education. The facility would include laboratories, areas for hazardous chemical research, and plant and animal support facilities. The equipment would include electron microscopes, atomic absorption spectrophotometers, amino acid analyzers, and nuclear magnetic resonance machines. Forty scientists from various disciplines would work there, able to easily communicate and share information among themselves.

Ground breaking ceremonies for the new Purdue animal science research and teaching facilities was held in the fall of 1983. Participating in the ceremonies were: George Doup, retired IFB president; Bill Marvel, IFB legislative department director; Marion Stackhouse, IFB president; Dr. Steven Beering, Purdue president; Dr. Bernie Liska, Purdue school of agriculture dean. The facilities are located at the Purdue Baker Farms north of West Lafayette. The Indiana General Assembly appropriated $5 million in 1983 to begin construction.

The IFB supported Purdue in its request to the Indiana General Assembly for the funds to build this facility—and for a very good reason. In an editorial in February 1979, *The Hoosier Farmer* stated,

> We sometimes take our food supply for granted. Complacency or the thought that we no longer need basic or applied research will not help us solve many of the difficult problems facing us, including maintaining and even increasing our food supplies which we sometimes take for granted.

Funds were approved for construction of the new research facility, and the new Agricultural Research Building was dedicated in early 1983. It was a high tech facility, as demanded by the times, containing electron microscopy facilities, labs where hazardous biological research could be safely conducted, and a center for research into cell physiology. It also contained a portion of the university's department of entomology. The entire facility was able to assist Purdue in conducting the mission-oriented research that is critical to the health and growth of Indiana agriculture.

One example of farm research with practical applications conducted at Purdue was unveiled in 1981, after the energy crisis had ended but when the nation's focus was still on conserving energy. Agricultural engineers at the West Lafayette campus created a biomass furnace, which allowed farmers to dry corn with heat derived from the complete combustion of corn cobs. This furnace was developed as a joint project of the U. S. Department of Agriculture and Purdue engineers.

It was estimated by the project engineers that if all the corn cobs from the 1979 crop were collected and burned in this way, the resulting energy would have equalled 97 million barrels of oil or 5.7 billion gallons of propane. The cobs from one acre could provide enough energy to dry two acres of corn, with enough left over for other uses such as heating buildings.

Purdue University was not the only educational institution that assisted with agricultural education in the state. Indiana Vocational Technical College also had a strong relationship with Indiana farm families, although in a different way than Purdue.

Ivy Tech, as it came to be known, was founded in 1963 to offer a post-secondary education for those Hoosiers who did not want to attend college but desired further formal learning. It provides college-level, job-oriented training in various technical and vocational fields. Students can obtain an Associate in Applied Science degree, which is a two-year program, or a Technical Certificate in one year.

By 1990, Ivy Tech had become Indiana's third-largest college, with centers in 24 communities around the state. Unlike the state's other colleges, however, its programs are focused on manpower needs and can lead directly to employment in the student's chosen field. In order to meet this requirement, Ivy Tech depends upon the expertise and advice of a variety of sectors, including commercial, labor, education, agriculture, industry, and the public at large.

In 1961, Dr. John Hicks of Purdue created the original idea for such a school, which was greatly needed to meet a serious gap in Indiana education. He contacted Glenn Sample, IFB vice president and secretary/treasurer, to help him begin formulating plans for the new school. Thus began the IFB's long association with Ivy Tech.

Sample began by serving as chairman of the committee that formulated the original proposal for the college, which was officially created by the Indiana General Assembly in 1963. He then served as the agriculture representative on the school's first board of trustees. In 1975, he took early retirement

Dale Wicoff, Ivy Tech instructor in agricultural equipment technology, explained the new school to state education and Farm Bureau leaders. Beginning in 1971, the program gave students a thorough understanding of servicing, repair and maintenance of all types of agricultural equipment. Wicoff served as program director.

Glenn Sample, president of Indiana Vocational Technical Institute (Ivy Tech) and past IFB vice president/secretary, was guest speaker at Farm Bureau's District 8 meeting in 1978. Sample pointed out that Indiana Farm Bureau played a major role in the development and success of Ivy Tech. At the head table are from left: George Ruschhaupt, district director; Sample; Rita Yager, district woman leader; and Marvin Johnson, Rush County president.

from the IFB to become president of Ivy Tech. During his 31 years of service with the IFB, he had served as editor of *The Hoosier Farmer*, director of information and public relations, corporate secretary/treasurer, and finally vice president. He also served as vice president and director of the Farm Bureau Insurance Companies.

While the IFB was sad to lose Sample, the organization was also proud that he had been chosen for the college position. As an editorial in *The Hoosier Farmer* stated, "While farmers regret his leaving Farm Bureau's leadership team, they're proud to have a farmer at the helm of Indiana's fifth state university."

Sample served as president of Ivy Tech for five years, until he died on January 7, 1980.

The IFB association with Ivy Tech did not end with his death, however. The link has grown stronger through the years, as more and more farm residents have had to move into outside occupations, and as Ivy Tech has grown and expanded to meet the increasing educational and occupational needs of Hoosiers. Ivy Tech also offers courses directly related to agriculture, with courses of study like agricultural equipment technology. These kinds of courses have become important as farm technology has become more complex. They help train not only technicians for positions with agriculture and industrial equipment manufacturers and farm supply industries, but they also train farmers to repair their own equipment so crucial to efficient farm operation.

More than a decade after Sample's death, another IFB executive, Corporate Secretary Marvin Metzger, served on the Ivy Tech Foundation Board, first as member, then secretary, vice chairman, and chairman, from July 1990 to October 1997. During his tenure, a successful fund drive to endow teacher scholarships and a campaign to rename the administration building after Sample were completed.

In 1977, the IFB suffered the loss of another of its great leaders, through retirement. George Doup, of Columbus, headed the organization for 19 years. Even though he had reached the IFB's mandatory retirement age, he admitted that he was ready to step down.

Doup began his association with the IFB as a township director on the board of directors of the Bartholomew County Farm Bureau. In 1938-39, he served as an honorary member of the IFB board while he was serving as president of Indiana Rural Youth. In 1946, he was elected director from his home district, District 8, and in 1951 was hired to head the IFB's livestock department. The next year, he was named vice president and then elected president in 1957, following the retirement of Hassil Schenck.

When he retired from IFB Inc., he also retired from the Farm Bureau Insurance companies, the Producers Marketing Association, and the Indiana

Speaking to more than 350 young farmers at the AFBF young farmers and ranchers advisory committee meeting was IFB President George Doup in 1972. The meeting was held in Clarksville.

Agricultural Association, which he had headed as president. Among his many accomplishments during his years at the IFB, he headed the successful campaign to raise more than $200,000 for improvements to the 4-H Leadership Center near Lafayette. He also traveled to 15 foreign countries as an agricultural ambassador and businessman, and appeared before state and national legislative bodies to represent agricultural interests.

Under his leadership, the IFB added new departments and programs to deal with the changing face of agriculture. The local affairs program increased the IFB's effectiveness in dealing with local school and government problems. The Indiana Agricultural Marketing Association, created in 1961, made it possible for commodity groups to organize for orderly sales of their products and to bargain with processors. In order to meet the growing problems of the environment and to keep members informed about new environmental regulations, the IFB natural resources department was created in 1966. The next year, the IFB record keeping service was introduced. The Young Farmer program was launched in 1969, and the County Farm Bureau Newsletter program began in 1970.

A radio and TV studio was added when the IFB building was remodeled in 1971, which meant the organization could produce taped programs available for use around the state. And in 1973, the Property Protection Program was initiated. It offered a $500 reward for information leading to the conviction of those who damaged or stole the property of IFB members.

Some 56,000 Hoosiers petitioned the 1972 Indiana General Assembly and Governor Edgar Whitcomb for property tax relief. Signatures were gathered by county Farm Bureaus and given to the governor. Reviewing signatures were C. W. Stall, Information & Public Relations Department; Hollys Moon, Legislative Department; Glenn Sample, IFB vice president; and Stanley Poe, Education Department.

In the later 1970s, when it was estimated that up to $1 billion worth of farm machinery was stolen each year, the IFB introduced another anti-theft program linked with the Property Protection Program. Using special equipment they could purchase from their county Farm Bureau offices, farmers could mark their equipment and machinery with their driver's license number, or a federal tax number in the case of a farm corporation, to make it easier to track in case of theft. Even if the numbers were ground off after the machinery was stolen, special techniques were available to re-establish the numbers.

Sponsors of the program included Farm Bureau Insurance, Indiana Sheriff's Association, Indiana State Police, Future Farmers of America, County Extension Service, 4-H Clubs, and high school vocational agriculture departments.

Indiana was the fifteenth state to participate in this machinery identification program. They were all tied in with the computers of the FBI's National Crime Information Center.

During the Doup presidency, the IFB also accomplished a great deal on the legislative front, on both the federal and state levels. Nationally, they included defeat of the 1963 Wheat Referendum, movement from a government-dominated national farm program to a freer market system, the revision of the federal estate tax law in 1976, and delay of a project under which Chicago sewage would have been dumped in Northwest Indiana.

On the state level, accomplishments included settlement of the time zone question, legislative approval of the property tax relief package in 1973, and establishment of a state pesticide review board and applicators' licensing law. *The Hoosier Farmer* lauded Doup in a January 1977 editorial:

> During his period of leadership Farm Bureau's public power has expanded from fighting for "equality for agriculture" to fighting for agricultural leadership in the arena of public affairs.
>
> People don't join Farm Bureau lightly. They join because they feel the need for the educational, promotional, legislative and economic services offered. Best evidence of their approval of the good job done during the Doup administration of 19 years, is the fact that during that period membership has grown from 130,700 families to nearly double that number—240,125—for 1976.
>
> Doup has been a truly great farm and business leader.

Later in 1977, Doup was named the first Visiting Distinguished Agriculturist by Purdue's School of Agriculture. The program was meant to bring the outstanding people in agribusiness to the school's agriculture faculty and campus. Doup was an excellent choice as the first person to fill this role, bringing his 40 years of agricultural and business experience with him.

Newly elected IFB President Marion Stackhouse, greeted well wishers during a reception in his office. Delegates at the 58th annual meeting picked the 53-year old farmer to fill the remaining year of Doup's unexpired two-year term. Field staff extending congratulations to Stackhouse and wife Phyllis were from left: Gene Pflug, Jerry Couch, Frank Larsen, and Paul Hoffman.

Indiana Farm Bureau, a long-time sponsor of the Indiana State Fair's Farmers Day Parade, sponsored the 1977 float depicting the parade theme: "Agriculture – A Growing Business." Graphics cited Indiana as the first state in the nation to reach 250,000 members. Tractor driver was Clark Lewis, Information & Public Relations Division.

Doup had resigned at the 1976 annual meeting of the IFB. At that same meeting, Marion Stackhouse was elected the new president to fill the remaining year of Doup's two-year term.

Stackhouse's extensive experience in agriculture made him an excellent choice for the new IFB president. Before joining the IFB in 1950 as a field representative, he was a vocational agriculture teacher. He operated a 300-acre hog and grain farm. He was director of the IFB commodity department, a director of Indiana Soybean Association, and a member of the executive committee of the Indiana Pork Producers Association. He had also served as chairman of the Swine Disease Advisory committee for the State Board of Animal Health and of the Indiana Meat Industry Committee for the National Livestock and Meat Board.

After completing his first term, Stackhouse was re-elected as president in 1978. For a decade, he would remain at the helm of the state's largest and most influential farm organization, maintaining during times of rapid change the IFB's course to remain relevant to the lives and livelihood of Hoosier farmers. Under his leadership, the IFB had two banner membership years. In 1977 and 1978, it had the largest membership of any state Farm Bureau in the country, with 250,000 and 282,742 members, respectively.

Attending IFB's District 9 "Salute to Agriculture – 1977" were from left: Marion Stackhouse, IFB president; Eloise Mickel, district woman leader; Allan Grant, AFBF president; and Robert Williams, district director. It was Grant's second visit to the state since his election to the post in 1976.

George Doup waves to the crowd, as he and his wife Martha accept the Distinguished Service Award from AFBF President Allan Grant at the 1979 national convention in Miami Beach. Some 700 Hoosiers attended the 60th annual meeting.

Chapter Four

Anniversaries And Cooperation

In 1976, the Women's Department of the IFB celebrated its 50th anniversary. The Women's Department had been outlined in a state meeting in 1922, when farm women were told they "would hold up a mirror to the agricultural genius of the state." The women present at that meeting spoke out for better homes and schools, and a richer life for farm families. The women's program developed into the early Social and Educational Committee. Its numbers were small in the beginning, but they continued to grow and gain influence in the IFB. October 27, 1926 was the day the Social and Education Department, later to be called the Women's Department—and even later the Women's Division—became an official part of the IFB organizational structure.

As its original name stated, the Women's Department had the responsibility for the education programs of the IFB. They created special programs for schools, rural and urban, to inform the students of farm life and concerns. Some of these programs, particularly in recent years, are aimed at reminding non-farm children that the farm is the true source of their food, not the grocery store. The women made presentations to adult gatherings, including governmental bodies and civic groups, to "interpret" Farm Bureau philosophy and beliefs. They sponsored an extensive awards program and offered prizes in public speaking for Indiana Rural Youth and for Farm Bureau women. They gave scholarships. They created the Pet and Hobby Club for children up to age 10, a program unique to Indiana, that would take place at the same time as the adult county meetings as a way to encourage attendance by young farm couples. (It was renamed "Little Farmers" in 1995.) They dealt with health and safety issues on the farm and stressed the importance of home economics to farm family health and budgets.

Admiring the plaque presented to Indiana Farm Bureau's women's committee at the 1978 AFBF convention were from left: Mary Jane Smith, Clinton, Oklahoma; Lois Gross, IFB women's committee chair; and Marion Stackhouse, IFB president. During the convention Gross was elected chair of the AFBF women's committee.

There was another aspect to the Women's Department, conducted in less formal, but no less important, settings. According to *Stepping Stones for Today's Path*, a history of the IFB Women's Division,

> Many friendships were made over a cup of tea served by Farm Bureau women to town and city business and professional persons. They have shared farm experiences on tours set up for town visitors. City children have been brought into farm homes to establish a better understanding of the farm, and the farm families have learned about the interests of their guests. (pg. 8)

The Women's Department, comprised of women from throughout Indiana townships and counties, opened wider horizons to its members. While their homes and families were of paramount importance, many women involved in Women's Department duties had the opportunity to travel and have many experiences that otherwise would not have been available, particularly in the IFB's earlier years.

At first, the Women's Department concentrated on local issues, but they eventually widened their scope to national and even international events. And not every area of concern involved farming. For instance, in March 1973, *The Hoosier Farmer* published an article about women's legislative issues. Included were the Equal Rights Amendment to the Constitution, abortion, and the potential ban of phosphates from detergents. The article included comments from women members of the Senate and House of Representatives, all of whom had been asked to participate.

District 7 Farm Bureau members survey materials available during their 1979 Bloomington Mall display. (l. to r.) Joan Root, Knox County woman leader; Richard Boberg, Knox County president; Conrad Begeman, District 7 director; Billie Simpson, District 7 woman leader; and W. T. Anderson, Lawrence County FB president.

One important program of the Women's Department was the Speaker's Bureau. It was developed in 1980 as a way for the IFB to talk about agriculture and farm life with non-farm audiences, such as Kiwanis Clubs, Rotary, garden clubs, and sororities. That first year, the women speakers used three programs, "Amazing Maize," "Chewing the Facts," and "Food is More Than Something to Eat." Initially, each county had several representatives that could present these presentations to the targeted groups.

In that same year, the Women's Department created the Tractor Safety Program, specifically for women. County women leaders coordinated the program in their counties.

Just as the image of farming itself has changed over the years, so has the image of farm women. Not all of them are "just wives." Between 1982 and 1995, for instance, there was an 8.2 percent increase in the number of women farm operators and a 12.8 percent increase in acreage operated by women. The Women's Department recognized this fact when they changed the name of their annual contest from Farm Wife of the Year to Farm Woman of Achievement.

Allan Grant, AFBF president, (back to camera) made one of his first major appearances since his January 1976 election when he addressed the Indiana Farm Bureau women's conference. Back stage he visited with IFB President George Doup, center. To the left are Elmo Ray and Lawrence Holloway, district directors.

Twenty years ago (1979) Farm-City Festival was the precursor to Ag Day. Sponsored by Farm Bureau at the state and national levels, it was intended to promote the exchange of ideas and information between farmers, ranchers and consumers and business people. The traditional cow-milking contest was conducted at the Indianapolis City Market. Farm Bureau President Marion Stackhouse knew exactly what to do. Records were unavailable on contest placings.

Marion Stackhouse praised farm women and noted their importance to Farm Bureau programs in *The Hoosier Farmer* of June 1979. He wrote:

> Many of these same women who can tell the farmer's story well can also drive tractors in preparing fields for spring crops. Their efforts in going to town after parts, feeding their families, being good listeners when things don't go right and lending a helping hand with the livestock chores make these women the most valuable partners known in the world today. They can equal most executives in their endeavors, and many times, I am sorry to say, do not even receive a word of thanks. So let me say thanks, to Indiana farm ladies, for a job well done!

Those farm women who are wives are full partners with their husbands. As *Stepping Stones for Today's Path* states,

> American farm women must be heavy equipment operators, market forecasters, public relations agents, financial planners, accountants, mechanics and animal husbandry specialists. These farming skills are required in addition to their traditional responsibilities of managing a household and raising children. And, more and more farm women are working off the farm as well, providing additional income for the family. (pg. 10)

Lois Gross was director of the Women's Department from 1957-1978 and chair of the Women's Committee from 1957 to December 15, 1980. During that time, the governing body of the women's department was renamed the State Women's Committee. It was comprised of district woman leaders. In 1957, Gross was appointed by the IFB board of directors to fill the post of state chair of the Women's Committee and second vice president of the organization. The position had been left vacant by the death of Nellie Flinn.

For many years, Gross had served on a volunteer basis, but after the State Women's Committee was formed, the director of the Women's Department became a part-time, paid staff position. The department also funded another staff position for secretarial duties.

When Gross began serving as vice chairman of the American Farm Bureau Women's Committee in 1976, she had to travel extensively. When she became chair in 1978, she resigned her IFB position as director of the Women's Department, although she retained her two other positions with the IFB. Gross also became vice president and then chairman of the American Farm Bureau Women's Committee , a position she retained until January 1981.

Judith Carley was the first full-time employee hired as director of the Women's Department after Gross stepped down. Along with other department heads, she reported to President Stackhouse, and she coordinated work in the many area's of the women's activities, including health, safety, farm

During the Summer Council annual meeting for county woman leaders at the Indianapolis Zoo, Carol Hegel, IFB second vice president, and Marion Stackhouse ride a ponderous pachyderm.

product promotion, public relations, and legislation until 1990. Carley remained as director of the Women's Department until 1989, and Jane Abbott then accepted that position and remained there for a year. At that time, Carolyn Hegel, who had been elected in 1980 to serve as director-at-large, was named by the IFB board as IFB second vice president and chair of the State Women's Committee. She assumed the duties of director of the Women's Department. In 1999, she still held those responsibilities.

During Hegel's tenure, many changes that reflected the changing times occurred within the Women's Division. The department became increasingly more professional and more involved in the business of IFB, rather than simply holding the responsibility for what used to be called "women's issues," which revolved around the home and family. Hegel, who has a business background, is also second vice president of IFB, and a director-at-large, which gives her a seat on the Boards of all the Farm Bureau companies, including the insurance companies.

During the 1990s, the international work of the Women's Division changed. Previously the division had been aligned with a humanitarian group that worked on social projects in third world countries.

"We decided to use our International Fund to expand our members' knowledge of world agriculture and world trade. I had the opportunity, while serv-

Indiana Farm Bureau board members in 1976 were: (l. to r.) Bob Williams, Elmo Ray, Marion Cowan, Lawrence Holloway, Oris Bedenkop, Virgil Cline, George Doup, Lois Gross, George Neff, Harry Pearson, Lowell Collins, George Ruschhaupt, and Linville Bryant.

Members of the state Women's Committee in 1976 were: (l. to r.) Mrs. Ernest Gross, Churubusco; Mrs. Tom Hegel, Andrews; Mrs. Loren Matlock, Greenfield; Mrs. Webster Heck, Connersville; Mrs. James Hon, Florence; Mrs. Bob Grider, secretary; Mrs. Guy Gross, committee chairman; Mrs. Albert Michel, Chandler; Mrs. Pearl Fidler, Sullivan; Mrs. Glendon Herbert, Cloverdale; Mrs. James Hon, Florence; and Mrs. Edwin Olson, Winamac.

ing on the AFBF National Women's Committee, to travel to Western Europe," Hegel said. "Much to my surprise, I found farmers who produced high-quality crops and livestock and nations dealing with farm surplus just as we were. Instead of going and teaching them, I was the one who ended up being the student and learning the lesson."

She wanted the Farm Bureau members to have similar opportunities. "The State Women's Committee established the Agricultural Cultural Exchange (ACE) Ambassador Program," she said. "It funded foreign trips to various parts of the world for ten farm couples."

Upon their return, couples would present programs at district meetings to share with others what they had learned. Hegel indicated a wonderful side effect: "It brought several people, who prior to this program had not been active members, into leadership roles of our organization." In 1999, Farm Bureau's next set of ACE International Ambassadors was selected.

The Women's Department also greatly expanded its educational role under Hegel's guidance. A program called "Farming in the Classroom" brings farm men and women into grades kindergarten through fourth grade to tell the students about various aspects of agriculture and farm life. The Women's Department also hosts teachers workshops, and they work together to develop educational videos about agriculture, food products, and so on. The department has also taken advantage of new technology to expand its educational efforts, developing programs and activities on CD-ROMs and creating an Internet chat room for farm women.

Another organization celebrated its golden anniversary in 1976: the Indiana Farm Bureau Cooperative Association. On March 17 and 18, the IFBCA celebrated at the Indiana State Fairgrounds with a wide array of product demonstrations and exhibits, entertainment, and a keynote speech by Secretary of Agriculture, Earl Butz.

At the celebration, the IFBCA reported record sales of $695 million for 1975, which was quintuple the sales of five years earlier. In addition, net savings amounted to $25 million, with $16.5 million left after payment of federal taxes, which were returned to county associations as patronage refunds. This amount brought the 20-year total of patronage refunds to more than $50 million.

By this time, the IFBCA owned and operated the world's largest nitrogen complex, at Donaldson, Louisiana, and two phosphate plants at Bartow and Plant City, Florida. The Mt. Vernon, Indiana, refinery supplied fuel to nearly half of all Hoosier farmers. In its efforts to continue supplying fuel during the oil embargo, the plant had operated in 1973 at a modest net loss, something that was less important than farmers having enough fuel to meet their needs. The IFBCA was then utilizing nine trains with up to 100 cars, each of which could carry 100 tons of grain, to the Baltimore, Maryland, terminal for overseas shipment, as well as to ports in Indiana and Chicago.

In early 1978, the IFBCA moved into a new home in Indianapolis, located at 120 E. Market Street. The 12-story Indiana Building offered the cooperative association an additional 300,00 square feet of space.

Research work conducted by the IFBCA, along with Purdue University and the U. S. Department of Agriculture, during its half-century history had led to great improvements in the genetic and nutritional qualities of grains. Research had also led to improvements in animal and poultry production. Farmers Forage Research Cooperative at Battleground, Indiana, had developed new varieties of crops, such as Tempo, Weevil Check alfalfa, and various hybrids.

The IFBCA had also taken an active role in trying to shape government policy to meet agriculture's needs and to respond to consumer concerns over rising food prices. One sore spot was that cooperatives were coming under government attack as a monopoly. The IFBCA's attempt to purchase several chemical plants had been blocked by the Justice Department, and its grain-handling was also being investigated. The IFBCA and Farm Bureau found this disturbing, considering that five large grain companies had a lock on 85 percent of the exported grain and that cooperatives exported no more than 7

Marion Stackhouse, left, IFB president, accepted the Gold Star award from AFBF President Allan Grant during the 1978 national convention. Three gold stars were earned in membership, young farmers, and commodity marketing. A silver star was awarded for women's activities. During the convention Stackhouse was chosen to serve on the AFBF board of directors. Indiana also had the largest delegation of any state with 550 attendees.

Ralph and Dora Bishop were honored at the Hoosier Barrow Show banquet. Bishop, for many years, served as show manager. Two of the show sponsors were Indiana Farm Bureau and IFB affiliate Producers Marketing Association. Gene Shaver, right, PMA general manager, presented a token of appreciation to Bishop on behalf of the Barrow Show committee.

percent of the nation's grain. In his address to those gathered for the IFBCA 50th anniversary celebration, Harold Jordan, former general manager and then special assistant to the general manager of the IFBCA, declared,

> There are many people in American today who do not understand, believe or appreciate that they still have the most abundant, nutritious and wholesome supply of food ever to be found on the face of the earth at prices that are very reasonable compared to their income and compared to any place else in the world. And this is largely because of the efficiency of the individual family farm; and this kind of efficient agriculture cannot endure in our present day economic climate unless farmers are permitted to develop cooperative institutions strong enough to deal with the large corporate giants with whom they must deal or compete today. (*The Hoosier Farmer*, May 1976)

However, if farmers were to continue succeeding, they needed more than simply the "efficiency of the individual family farm." They also required efficient ways to market their products. The Indiana Agricultural Marketing Association continued to find ways to help Hoosier agricultural producers with this task. In 1976, the IAMA added a new division called the Indiana Farm Fresh Association (IFF) to assist those farmers who sold part of their produce at the retail level.

One of the first activities the IFF took on was the creation of an informational campaign to let consumers know about Farm Fresh locations, where farmers sold portions of their produce directly to the customer. In order to maintain high standards of cleanliness, the IFF also inspected and certified Farm Fresh locations. Members were kept informed with a newsletter. They were also offered services in record keeping, market layout, and business tips. The IAMA sponsored various workshops for Farm Fresh market operators, fruit and vegetable growers who sold their products at roadside stands or country markets.

The IAMA continued to expand and improve its other programs for producers of popcorn, tomatoes, and poultry. Several meetings held every year allowed producers the opportunity to become better acquainted with IAMA programs, to discuss production and marketing problems, and to become informed about current farm issues.

The IAMA operated with the same board and officers as the IFB. It also received staff help from the IFB commodity department and field services staff. The IAMA also contributed input to many IFB conferences, offering information on topics like farm transportation, farm labor, grain rate-making, and futures markets and prices.

This kind of cooperation was typical throughout the entire IFB organization. From the very beginning, members knew that working together would take them farther than would working separately. For instance, policy development involves Farm Bureau members throughout the year and culminates in the adoption of the group's state policy at the annual state convention. Here is how this process works:

The policy development begins at the county level, where appointed committees are asked to meet regularly throughout the year to review previous policies, determine new issues, conduct research, and discuss possible new policy. These committee members attend a wide range of meetings related to agriculture.

The county committees prepare policy recommendations to present at the county annual fall meetings. Local policies remain within the counties, while those recommendations with state and national ramifications are sent to the State Policy Development Committee, also known as the Resolutions Committee.

The members of the State Policy Development Committee are appointed by the state president. It represents the IFB's 10 state districts, the Young Farmer Committee, the Women's Committee, and two advisory members from the state board of directors.

The November 1976 IFB resolutions committee considered county Farm Bureau recommendations. They were: (l. to r.) Front row: Eugene Lamb, Randolph; Everett Kirkendall, Clinton; Betty Mosely, Miami; Rosalind Kitchel, Wayne; Larry Pflug, Gibson; and Earl Bray, Switzerland. Back row: Harry Pearson, district director; LeRoy Lowe, Jay; Virgil Cline, IFB vice president and resolutions committee chairman; George Hadley, Hendricks; Bernard Schantz, Greene; Mike Zimmerman, Kosciusko; David Leising, Franklin; Buford Drake, Franklin; Francis Nelson, DeKalb; Robert Williams, district director; and Richard Smith, Marshall.

President George Doup, right, stood with the director of a commune in the Shanghai area. His 1976 visit to what was then called "Red China" was part of the "opening door China policy" to encourage American interest in United States. Doup commented, "Hopefully in the years ahead, China will open her borders for increased trade with the United States. This country can, in time, become a good market for some of our agricultural production and a valuable trading partner. The food and other needs of a nation of 800 million cannot be ignored."

The county committees send their recommendations to the state committee, which categorically modifies and discusses them. Resolution categories are Commodity, Marketing and Regulatory Functions; Education; Health, Safety and Welfare; Membership Participation; Natural Resources; State and Local Government; Miscellaneous; and National and International.

Once the state resolutions committee has acted upon the counties resolutions, they are prepared for distribution to all state delegates to review before

the state convention. During the convention, the delegates and the state committee discuss the resolutions and make amendments and deletions. The recommendations that are approved at the delegate session become IFB policy for the coming year; later, complete policy books are offered to members via an order coupon in *The Hoosier Farmer.* National and international recommendations are forwarded to the AFBF Resolutions Committee for consideration during the national convention's delegate session.

The process begins once again the day after the state convention ends. The Policy Development committee members work to keep citizens around the state of Indiana informed and educated about the problems affecting farmers. They are assisted in this effort by a variety of resources, including state advisory committees, county committees for commodity, local affairs, natural resources, women, and other interests; Farm Bureau publications; speakers; and local school and government personnel and resources.

Cooperation among farmers extended even beyond national borders. The IFB often sent representatives on trade missions or other trips to foreign countries. In 1977, for instance, Stanley Poe, IFB education department director, was asked to participate in a seminar on farm cooperatives in Brasilia, Brazil. He was accompanied by other agricultural experts from around the country. Cooperative personnel from all states in Brazil attended the seminar, and later that same year, they came to the United States to visit cooperatives, including several in Indiana.

During 1976, Doup traveled to China to visit with farmers there. With a staggering 800 million mouths to feed, China, only slightly larger than the United States, produces its food on 11 percent of its land. By comparison, the U.S., with less than 200 million inhabitants, farmed 20 percent of its land during the same time period. In many areas of China, he found, the weather allows double and triple cropping of rice and wheat— and many vegetables produce an amazing five crops a year.

Marion & Phyllis Stackhouse were part of the AFBF trade mission to Israel, May 1977. Among the many sites visited was an experimental farm specializing in varieties and disease control in wheat. The group was a guest of the Israeli government and farm organizations. After returning, Stackhouse wrote: "Because of Israel's location and importance in the political world, and its total dependence on the United States for livestock feed, our farmers will have a vital impact on their government and success."

Doup visited three Peoples Communes, in Beijing, Shanghai, and Kwangchow, and found that the commune structure includes agriculture, industry, trade, schools, and hospitals, as well as all other service programs. Upon his return, he wrote,

> Hopefully, in the years ahead, China will open her borders for increased travel and trade with the United States. This country can, in time, become a good market for some of our agricultural production and a valuable trading partner. The food and other needs of a nation of 800 million cannot be ignored. (*The Hoosier Farmer*, December 1976)

In May 1977, Marion Stackhouse traveled with the AFBF on a trade mission to Israel. He saw first hand how necessary it was for the U. S. to continue farm product export expansion. At that time, the Israelis were importing 1.1 million tons of feed grain, 500,000 tons of wheat, and 350,000 tons of soybeans, mainly from the United States. With a population of 3.5 million, they couldn't grow enough food in their tiny country, much of which was desert.

By the end of the trip, Stackhouse had discovered that

> The [Israeli] farmers are hard working and very modern and innovative. They are using late model, United States 4-wheel drive tractors and late model United States combines, because of their ability to put the farming operations of several together into a unit large enough to use such equipment.
>
> Because of Israel's location and importance in the political world, and its total dependence on the United States to feed its livestock population, our farmers will have a vital impact on their government and success. (*The Hoosier Farmer*, July 1977.)

The next year, he participated in a trade mission to the Soviet Union, the purpose of which was to help sell grain to the Soviets. This was the first "farmer to farmer" trade mission conducted between the U.S. and the U.S.S.R. While the trade mission representatives, who also included two other American Farm Bureau board members, a foreign trade expert, and two representatives from Cargill, did not have the opportunity to talk with anyone involved in the purchasing of wheat, corn, or soybeans, they spent a great deal of time with Russian farmers and others directly involved in agricultural production.

Stackhouse felt that this trip was very effective in terms of learning more about the Soviet system of collective farming and understanding the needs of Soviet farmers and consumers. He did say, though, that trade negotiations would continue to be difficult because the Soviet government was not forthcoming about its plans for agriculture or for importing foodstuffs from the United States.

Back at home, the IFB continued its opposition to government legislation it considered wrong-headed or detrimental to farmers and agriculture. One such bit of legislation was the creation of the Consumer Protection Agency, which the IFB viewed as redundant. In his column in the October 1977 *The Hoosier Farmer*, Stackhouse stated flat-out, "The Consumer Protection Agency concept is wrong." He gave many reasons why he and many IFB members believed that was the case:

> Sponsors of the bill for the agency say it would represent the interests of the consumer in federal agency proceedings. If that is true, this indicates the failure of federal agencies to do the job they were supposed to do in the first place...
> Why are taxpayers being told they need to pay for another agency just because the ones they are already financing are not doing their jobs?
> We firmly believe the people are being told this because the bureaucracy is out of control. The people should be told that the administration and Congress do not know how to solve this problem from within the existing agencies, so how can they handle this with a new agency?...
> If any private organization were to pay people for not performing their jobs, the result would be the eventual ruin of the organization.

The IFB had long sought to make louder the voice of the farmer in national affairs to ensure that the voice was not drowned out by louder or more insistent voices who did not understand the facts of agricultural life. In order to more effectively mobilize Indiana farmers on important national matters that could affect them, the IFB created the National Affairs Department in 1977. Don Henderson, director of the Organization Department, was tapped to head National Affairs.

As an example of the focus of the National Affairs Department, Henderson wrote an article for the January 1978 issue of *The Hoosier Farmer* reminding farmers about their stake in international trade. At that time, representatives from many countries were gathered in Geneva, Switzerland, for the seventh round of negotiations on the General Agreement on Tariffs and Trade (GATT). The importance of GATT to farmers in Indiana, as Henderson wrote, is that it "is the only multi lateral trade agreement which lays down an agreed code of rules for the fair conduct of world trade," including the sales of agricultural products. He pointed out these facts:

> In 1972 the U. S. had $8 billion in ag exports, in 1976 this had increased to $26 billion. We currently export 55% of our wheat, 52% of our soybeans and 27% of our corn. Drop these percentages by even 1 or 2% and one quickly sees what happens to the market price as stocks build up...

A "who's who" in Farm Bureau headed towards the White House for a meeting with officials concerning grain surpluses. (l. to r.) Marion Stackhouse, IFB president; Harold Steele, Illinois FB president; Allan Grant, AFBF president; C. R. Johnson, Missouri FB president; and Dean Kleckner, Iowa FB president. They were part of the eight FB officers taking part in a meeting with Stuart Eizenstat, U.S. President Jimmy Carter's domestic policy advisor, and Lynn Daft, presidential assistant. The delegation reported to the administration that grain surpluses posed a serious threat to agriculture and urged that an acreage set-aside program limiting the corn crop to 5.5 billion bushels in 1979 be announced as soon as possible.

If export markets are to be expanded with the current round of negotiations it will be necessary for those representing agriculture to monitor the negotiations carefully and speak forcefully in agriculture's behalf. The American Farm Bureau has a staff expert on international trade in Geneva, Switzerland, at the present time to relay to AFBF important happenings as they occur.

Henderson and the National Affairs Department remained abreast of further developments in foreign trade. The 1978 Agricultural Trade Expansion Act, passed by the 95th Congress, signalled important opportunities for the foreign sales of American agricultural products. It authorized new Commodity Credit Corporation programs, some of which would help with agricultural sales in China, a new export market for the United States.

The importing and exporting of agricultural products is a complex business, and the huge grain sales of the 1970s often grabbed major headlines and created a great psychological impact on those who did not understand their importance to not only U. S. farmers but the entire economy. The IFB Commodity Department of the 1970s took pains to explain to members how the markets worked.

For instance, in the May 1979 issue of *The Hoosier Farmer*, Gary Pursifill of the Commodity Department wrote the article, "Who Are The Exporters and Importers?" He explained that the export business "is very volatile. On

U.S. Senator Richard Lugar, discussed ag policy before the finals of the Young Farmer discussion meet at the 1979 IFB convention. Standing in the background is Marion Stackhouse, IFB president. Participants were Thomas Buis, Putnam; Bob Kissel, Hancock; Tom Malsch, moderator; Jerry Frey, Carroll; and Don Villwock, Knox. Judges selected Villwock over-all winner.

any given year, one country may have a shortage and become a very big buyer. The next year that same country may buy very little." Because of these frequent shifts, he explained that it was important to take a long-range view of the markets. Even at that time, when America exported 30 percent of its corn, more than 40 percent of its beans, and even more of its wheat, he said, "We have only scratched the surface in the area of creating export demand for our farm products."

In 1979, the IFB joined with the IFBCA, several other American co-ops, and four European co-ops to form a limited partnership to help with international exports and sales. The partnership purchased 50 percent interest in an international grain marketing firm called Alfred C. Toepfer International GmbH, of Hamburg, West Germany. The firm was 60 years old and had 43 offices in 17 countries. At that time, it was trading 18 to 20 million metric tons per year.

Glenn Franklin, executive vice president of the IFBCA, explained in an article in *The Hoosier Farmer* why this move into the international commodity market was so important:

> ...the Alfred C. Toepfer International GmbH can source grains from anywhere in the world, providing the critical flexibility required to compete effectively for export sales, which is a market position that Indiana farmers have been working toward for a long time. The acquisition will give the Cooperative immediate, direct access to vital trading intelligence and access to distant markets. (February 1980)

The IFB took this action to provide Indiana farmers with a little, direct piece of the international trade market. However, the purchase was also an indirect response to critics of the sale of U. S. grain to the Soviet Union, who were very active at that time. Such sales actually helped guarantee adequate food production in the U. S. and helped keep it available at reasonable prices. Marion Stackhouse explained how in the December 1979 issue of *The Hoosier Farmer*:

> If the American farmer cannot dispose of surplus products (these products not needed to supply the domestic market) there will need to be a substantial cutback in U. S. agricultural production, as currently $2 of every $5 gross farm income in Indiana comes from foreign markets. If our production is going to have to be contracted, per unit cost could far exceed that of a more normal full production concept. It is totally unacceptable for agriculture to ignore this market demand. The only exception would be if prices are so low that many farmers would go bankrupt. Large expenditures of government money would be necessary to sustain U. S. agriculture and there would be no

During a 1979 AFBF board of directors meeting in Washington, D.C., with the Senate Agricultural Committee, Senator Richard Lugar, second from left, greets Allan Grant, AFBF president. To the left are Lois Gross, IFB second vice president and AFBF Women's committee chair; and Marion Stackhouse, IFB president.

profit or earnings for the farmer to spend for his necessities and less investment capital to produce the next year's agriculture crop.

Stackhouse reported that, during the Soviet grain embargo in 1980 (a federal response to the USSR's invasion of Afghanistan), other countries were wondering why the U.S. government would take such action. He told the 62nd annual IFB convention about his recent trip to Argentina, where,

> ...their first question to us was, "What is the new administration going to do about the embargo?" It might amaze some of you to know that they too want the embargo lifted as we do. This may be hard to understand when they admit they have sold coarse grains into world trade for about $50 a ton premium because our country was trying to deny this grain to Russia and other countries.
> I specifically asked these people why they supported taking the embargo off, and they indicated that it was incidental, a small item in world politics. They want the U. S. to again assume the leadership role in the free world, and they think that America cannot assume this role as long as they play the embargo game.

Those in attendance at the convention also heard from Michael Calingaert, assistant secretary of state for international resources and food policy, who outlined the Reagan administration's policy regarding agricultural exports. In the previous few decades, grain had become an important aspect of the global political scene, since an adequate food supply was one way of avoiding unrest. He concluded his presentation by saying:

> ... grain has assumed a major role in U. S. foreign economic policy. It is woven into the fabric of our relations with countries all around the world. Grain is on the agenda of international meetings in New York, Rome, London, and Africa. The international importance of grain is not likely to decline in the foreseeable future. Quite the contrary, given the high existing levels of trade, global population growth and lagging agriculture in many developing countries, there will be increasing global demand for grain. The problems generated by growth in demand are likely to intensify international discussion of food and agricultural policy in the decades of the eighties. The United States will be participating in these discussions, working to advance both the interests of its producers and its overall foreign policy interests. (*The Hoosier Farmer*, February 1981)

If anyone had doubted the importance of American—and Hoosier—foodstuffs to world peace and economics, these words would help them understand. The IFB and its sister Farm Bureaus throughout the country continued their fight for an expanding international grain market free of government interference.

Indiana Lt. Governor & Governor Elect Robert D. Orr, welcomed Farm Bureau and Cooperative members at the December 1979 joint convention. The 61st annual meeting was combined to add emphasis to Farm Bureau membership and the crucial role of the state Farm Bureau cooperative. The convention theme was "Stepping into the 1980s."

Chapter Five
Government Intervention

The 1980s opened with a prediction from the American Farm Bureau Federation that net farm income for 1980 was expected to drop $34.8 billion and that net farm cash receipts would be reduced by 25 percent—not a very good way to begin a new decade. But as it had done for the past six decades, the IFB continued to advocate for Indiana's farmers, whatever the economic backdrop.

This depressing financial picture was the result, in large part, of federal government action. The grain embargo against the Soviet Union in protest of its invasion of Afghanistan had led to 17 million tons of grain being put back on the market, causing a domestic glut that resulted in drastically lower prices. (To make matters worse, the embargo was declared a failure in terms of putting economic pressure on Russia.) In response to this situation, Editor Tom Asher wrote in *The Hoosier Farmer*:

> ... farmers and their organizations make it quite clear that food must not become a political weapon to be used casually at the whim of politicians for political reasons. Why? Because it affects the very lives, well being and security of our own U. S. citizens—farmers and ranchers. It is not an action that farmers will tolerate if grain embargoes become commonplace. (March 1980)

In addition to its opposition to government intervention in the agricultural marketplace, the IFB continued its protests against the growing trend of federal government intervention in many areas of life at the expense of states' rights and the rights of individuals.

For example, Lois Gross, who was chairman of the American Farm Bureau Women's Committee, IFB second vice president, and chairman of the State Women's Committee in the early 1980s, spoke to the U.S. House of

Representatives on the matter of compulsory national health insurance. She reiterated the Farm Bureau policy to the House Ways and Means Subcommittee on Health: "We believe reliance should be placed mainly upon the private sector to solve the financial aspects of health care problems. Further government intervention in the financing of health care will not be helpful either to the citizens or the health care system." (*The Hoosier Farmer*, April 1980)

Farm Bureau had its own recommendations, which Gross also related to the committee: that Congress enact legislation to grant federal income tax credits for premiums paid for health care plans, and that the self-employed be permitted a tax deduction as a business expense for the full cost of health insurance premiums.

The question of food additives had arisen in full force in the 1970s and continued into the 1980s. One of the major battles was over nitrites in bacon

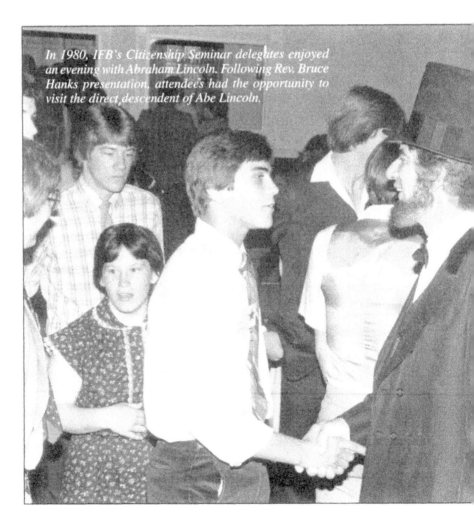

In 1980, IFB's Citizenship Seminar delegates enjoyed an evening with Abraham Lincoln. Following Rev. Bruce Hanks presentation, attendees had the opportunity to visit the direct descendent of Abe Lincoln.

and processed meats. A study done at the Massachusetts Institute of Technology and publicized by the USDA and the Food and Drug Administration had shown—many said inconclusively—that nitrites and nitrosamines caused cancer in the lymphatic systems of test animals. In November 1978, both Marion Stackhouse and Will Schakel, director of the IFB Commodity Department, wrote in *The Hoosier Farmer* that a ban on nitrites would threaten the hog industry—without adequate proof of harm.

Stackhouse told a Senate committee that the USDA plan to phase in a ban on nitrites had not been subjected to scientific peer review and had even been dubbed "inconclusive" by its author. More than 60 percent of all pork was processed with nitrite preservatives, and processed meats accounted for $12 billion in retail sales annually. He said if the ban was carried out, it would "have a significant impact on the availability of widely used meat products, on the prices paid by consumers for these products and on the incomes received by livestock producers."

He asked Congress that no further steps be taken to ban nitrites until further studies had been carried out, and that adequate funding be provided for the development of suitable, effective substitutes. He concluded his testimony by saying,

> ...we hope that members of Congress and top officials in government agencies will refrain from public comments that can be construed as scare tactics. If research proves that such attacks are unwarranted, a great injustice will have been done to many innocent, hardworking tax-paying Americans, especially those thousands of farmers and ranchers whose markets are being threatened without just cause.

Schakel echoed those sentiments in his article, saying that "we are facing a most serious new threat." He explained that a ban on nitrites would mean that

> ...present technology cannot produce bacon, smoked and canned hams, smoked picnics, smoked butts and the hundreds of varieties of lunch meats as we now know them. Until new types of cures win consumer acceptance, practically all pork cuts and trimmings would probably have to be marketed at sharply

During a 1978 visit to Washington, D.C., Don Henderson, IFB National Legislative Affairs Department director, delivered hundreds of letters to U.S. Senator Richard Lugar. The letters were written by Hoosiers opposed to the proposed nitrate reduction for bacon and the proposal to limit antibiotics in animal feeds.

reduced prices with the exception of loins, butts and spare ribs. This could drop hog prices to disastrous low levels, forcing a major reduction in the hog herd.

But the biggest threat would be a tremendous human health problem in the form of botulism. This is a very real problem that could include much sickness and possibly death...

We believe nitrites do not affect consumers and that the risks of botulism, changes in cooking and eating habits and the higher costs, far outweigh the idea of removing nitrites from the market.

Many others weighed in on the side of pork producers and the IFB. Among them was Sen. Richard Lugar of Indiana, a member of the Senate Agriculture Committee. He said the hearings raised serious questions about the data so far collected. He warned federal agencies against banning the use of nitrites as preservatives in meat, particularly when Congress was not in session, without further evidence that they were linked to cancer. He agreed with Schakel that the ban would subject consumers to increased chances of botulism, as well as higher prices and "severe dislocations for pork producers." He also said that seven pages of the FDA report containing information on deficiencies in the study were left out of copies handed out to consumer groups. The "missing pages in other copies leave some doubt as to the FDA's intentions," he stated.

The next year, the nitrite controversy continued. In late 1979, Assistant Secretary of Agriculture Carol Tucker Foreman spoke to members of the Bartholomew County Farm Bureau and the Columbus (Indiana) Chamber of Commerce and answered a question about nitrites. The USDA was at that time waiting for final reports on the MIT study. According to *The Hoosier Farmer*, she said, "No one will be happier for the current studies to be positive. We would very much like for the nitrite problem to go away but I honestly don't think it will."

Giving another view of the situation, she said,

Nine months ago we told bacon manufacturers that they would have to manufacture bacon that could be shown to have less than 10 parts per billion nitrosamines. The bacon manufacturers said they would go out of business, we can't do it. It has been nine months and every bacon manufacturer in the U.S. is still manufacturing bacon. Not one has gone out of business. People who like bacon can eat it knowing they are not getting a cancer causing substance in their bacon.

In 1980, the USDA and Food and Drug Administration decided that nitrites would not be removed from food. One witness at a 1980 Congressional hearing on nitrites, at which Marion Stackhouse spoke on behalf of the AFBF, estimated that "the government's actions on nitrites adversely affected bacon over a billion dollars," according to *The Hoosier Farmer* (November 1980). The IFB offered its thanks to Sen. Lugar and others who worked on behalf of farmers to prevent the ban from going into effect before all the facts were in. The IFB, via Marion Stackhouse, called on government officials to have accurate information before they issued such proclamations. As an example of the ways citizens were losing faith in their government, he recalled his experience at the 1978 Congressional hearings on nitrites:

> ...the government people were not even in the mood to listen. They thought they had a piece of information that was quite newsworthy, and they played it to the hilt. It was disturbing to me when the congressional people questioned those involved and they flatly denied all these allegations. I feel I would have more respect for these government people if they would not use flimsy arguments, and the law, and many new regulations of open files, full disclosures, and many other laws to restrict producers who are important to our society...
>
> It is well known that we have many people who fear the product now because of this experience, and they will not eat bacon even though it has been declared safe. The demand side must be recognized as well as the production side. I am afraid here lies one of the great faults of our government listening to groups with an ax to grind without full understanding of the economics of the issues involved. (*The Hoosier Farmer*, November 1980)

Like it or not, the nitrites episode, along with grain embargoes and labor strikes, demonstrated how closely food was tied into politics. By 1980, the U.S. was supplying nearly $40 billion worth of agricultural products to the world outside its borders. Stackhouse said, "The farmers and agricultural business leaders of our nation have been almost geniuses in their ability to solve production and marketing problems as they organize the elevators, the transportation and the marketing facilities around the world." (*The Hoosier Farmer*, December 1980) He called again on the government to let these "almost geniuses" continue their work unmolested by further regulation or holding food hostage to politics: "The American private market system can deliver this more efficiently that our government can."

Another thing that farmers could deliver efficiently was petroleum products, via the IFBCA and its system of a refinery, oil wells, and transportation networks. After its success in supplying adequate fuel supplies during the energy crisis in the previous decade, the IFBCA continued its work in the 1980s. The IFBCA had become deeply involved in programs that would ensure the availability of petroleum products and other fuels to its farmer-patrons, including gasohol and other alternative fuels. These new programs had been developed without undue price increases.

Indiana Farm Bureau leaders traveled to Washington, D.C., to promote ag issues such as repeal of the Delaney Clause, USDA reorganization and inflation. Senator Birch Bayh spent time with the national affairs coordinators in explaining current (1978) legislation that was going to affect Indiana agriculture.

National legislative coordinators developed insight on practical ways to effectively voice policy positions during stays in Washington, D.C. In 1978, Senator Richard Lugar explained current legislative issues and then fielded questions from the Indiana delegation.

Indiana Farm Bureau's officers and board of directors in 1980 were: (l. to r.) Harold Myers, Harry Pearson, Lowell Collins, Ralph Ponsler, Randall Walker, Virgil Cline, Marion Stackhouse, Lois Gross, Robert Willliams, Conrad Begeman, Elvin Ashwill, Lawrence Holloway, and Wayne Emigh.

As a result of the energy crisis, the IFBCA realized that the competitive leverage in the oil industry was no longer in refinery capacity, but in ownership of crude oil. So the IFBCA began its own exploration for new oil fields. In 1980 alone, the IFBCA drilled 160 domestic holes in search of crude oil, 85 of which were developed into commercial oil wells. Most of these were located in the Illinois Basin, which supplied the Mt. Vernon refinery with most of its crude oil. By 1980, the refinery was capable of producing 22,000 barrels a day of a variety of petroleum products, including diesel fuel, heating oils, gasoline, and liquid propane gas. Its storage tanks held 63 million gallons of crude oil and large quantities of liquid propane.

Because it was important to keep expensive farm machinery in excellent working condition, the IFBCA also developed and produced a full line of lubricants and motor oils.

The IFBCA had developed an excellent delivery system over the years to get its products to its customers. A pipeline 238 miles long carried finished petroleum products from the Mt. Vernon refinery to Peru, Indiana The pipeline terminals at Switz City, Jolietville, and Peru allowed the products to be sent on to the member association bulk plants. From these terminals, petroleum transport trucks carried the fuel to customers.

Since domestic oil could not supply 100 percent of the demand, the IFBCA also purchased foreign oil. In one case, the IFBCA joined with 15 other cooperatives to acquire a concession to drill a hole in Egypt. The IFBCA then joined with several partners to form Agri-Petco International, which acquired a license to explore for crude offshore from Ghana, West Africa.

This integrated system of fuel production and delivery "assures farmer-patrons of complete control of every phase of operation so that they are being served with the best products at the lowest possible cost." (*The Hoosier Farmer*, December 1980)

The IFBCA also improved its grain accounting procedures in 1980, using a new computer system. According to *The Hoosier Farmer* of May 1980, the new system

> ...makes grain accounting swifter, surer and easier. In addition, the system keeps management of the farm cooperative fully informed of up-to-date grain positions—something that is increasingly vital if the cooperative is to best serve its farmer patrons and grain-buying customers.

The computers were placed at the county co-op facilities to keep track of receipts, transactions, inventories, prices, and shipments, as well as supply and management information, on a daily basis. All the county computers were tied into the main computer in Indianapolis to facilitate month-end and year-end data processing.

The computerized system drastically reduced the amount of paperwork previously required to handle all the grain accounting functions. Prior to the system installation, each transaction had to be handled manually many times. The process involved numerous steps, which became a "nightmare at harvest" for the office staff, according to Joe Latham, general manager of the Vigo County Farm Bureau Cooperative, who was quoted in *The Hoosier Farmer*. Even with working 16- or 17-hour days, they could not keep up, resulting in out-of-date information. However, with the computer system installed, one clerk, working only a little overtime, was able to handle the entire workload. The farmer patrons were also happy with the new system since it enabled them to receive their settlement checks more quickly than in the past.

In 1981, the IFBCA offered a $10 million debenture bond offering to acquire sufficient cash to continue expanding and improving its facilities. This sale was made necessary by the high cost of money at the time and the IFBCA's recent capital expenditures. The bonds were available for sale to all Indiana residents, and the bonds were to be honored before any payments or distributions were made to stockholders and patrons. Those expenditures included the $20 million renovation of the deep water shipping terminal at Locust Point, Maryland, acquisition of an interest in A. C. Toepfer International, foreign expansion of crude oil supplies, and integration of its fertilizer supply through CF Industries, as well as the cost of maintaining an adequate inventory of its products.

The A. C. Toepfer investment was an interesting series of events. Some of the investment dollars were provided by Farm Bureau Insurance to the

U.S. Senator Dan Quayle hosted IFB officers and board of directors in Washington, D.C. During the 1981 trip, key issues discussed were inflation, President Ronald Reagan's economic recovery plan, the farm program, estate taxes, exports and the Russian grain embargo.

In 1981, Indiana Farm Bureau's board of directors listened to USDA Secretary John Block. He talked about the severe impact of the Russian grain embargo on U.S. farmers. They also met with Indiana's U.S. Senators Quayle and Lugar.

Indiana Farm Bureau Cooperative Association to help finance the expansion into foreign markets. The dollars passed from Insurance through Indiana Farm Bureau to IFBCA in a rare night board meeting of Indiana Farm Bureau.

All this activity was taking place against the backdrop of a very bad financial time for Indiana farmers. Parity in 1980 came close to being the worst ever. Starting out at 65, it fell to 63 and then to 60 in April, the lowest parity since April 1933. It rose again for several months, averaging out to 64 for the year, making 1980 the second worst year (along with 1934) in IFB history. At the same time, farm debt rose by about 15 percent each year over the last four years, while the dollar decreased in value. In 1980, cash farm receipts rose by 6.9 percent while cost outlays soared to nearly 11 percent.

High inflation was also having a serious impact on agriculture, particularly through interest rates. Facing increased interest costs plus high amounts of funds needed for capital investment, farmers were caught between the proverbial rock and a hard place, with costs overshadowing any margins on most farm products. The beef industry was hard hit, with losses as high as $120 per animal, as was the hog sector, with hogs selling at $10 losses for a time. Proposed tax spending was threatening to drive inflation even higher, leading the IFB to call for new levels of farm prices if farmers were not to go bankrupt.

In addition, the IFB agreed with the national economic recovery plan. This plan called for 10 percent tax cuts in 1981, 1982, and 1983, reducing spending by cutting waste, revising entitlements and streamlining bureaucracy, and eliminating unnecessary regulation. It was estimated that these moves would balance the national budget in three years (although this did not occur until 1998).

At the height of this poor economic situation, Congress was considering the 1981 farm bill. One difficulty was that farmers themselves held differing opinions about what the bill should include. Many of those farmers who were in difficult financial straits wanted the government to prop up the agricultural economy, while those farmers who were more fortunate did not desire such assistance. The IFB agreed that, while some farmers needed help, it was best for the government to take the least amount of control possible.

As usual, the IFB took a critical look at the proposed bill and presented an opinion. They offered a few additional amendments that they believed would bring some stability to the ag sector while not raiding the federal treasury, yet coinciding with demands in the world market and increasing farm income.

Marion Stackhouse summed up the IFB position on the proposed farm bill in the October 1981 issue of *The Hoosier Farmer*. It contained what the IFB, now the largest state Farm Bureau organization in the country, had long advocated:

> Indiana Farm Bureau is not opposed to farmers being paid a
> reasonable amount for their crops. We are reluctant to step into a

trap where other people determine our economic well being. Our delegates have pointed us in the direction of keeping a long time, sound arena for agriculture to operate in rather than get caught up in a short time, politically motivated bail out.

In his speech to the delegates gathered at the 63rd annual meeting, Stackhouse reiterated that troubled times are the times when farmers need their organization the most. The knowledge, expertise, and dedication of the IFB members and leaders are some of the most valuable assets of the group, he told those assembled, and it is those qualities that come to the fore when bad times hit.

He believed that the 1980s would be more conservative for farmers than the previous decade. Farmers probably would not be able to continue assuming the same financial risks, largely because high inflation made that a poor choice. He said,

> It was one thing for farmers to leverage when the value of what was leveraged was going up faster than inflation rates, but a new ballgame when the interest rates are higher and more costly than the value of their leveraged item. This creates a negative drain on their investments and it is a major problem facing the farmers today.

Just as farmers had to tighten their belts, so did government, he declared. Entitlement programs needed to be trimmed, and money spent more wisely on both the federal and state levels. He also called for the U.S. government to take another look at how American agriculture products could be put back into demand by foreign countries. While the Soviet Union needed grain, they were loathe to buy any from American farmers, in retaliation for the previous U.S. grain embargo against them. (Sen. Richard Lugar introduced a bill in the summer of 1982 that would prevent the federal government from interfering with existing export contracts in the event of another embargo.) Stackhouse said that grain was being used as a weapon to prevent the Soviets from invading Poland and commented,

> We recognize that food is one of the strongest assets of our nation. We only hope that the State Department will use the farmers and the food industry as an incentive for a better world, and particularly peace, rather than as a club which causes other nations to retaliate.

In one effort to improve the foreign trade situation, some of the leadership and staff of the American Farm Bureau and the IFB traveled to Washington to talk with the Secretary of Agriculture and the U. S. Trade Representative about assistance with stimulating overseas sales of value-added agricul-

A 1982 IFB state women's committee program was "Make Ends Meat." Some 100 central Indiana home ec teachers received updates on the food story and supporting materials available through IFB and the Cooperative Extension Service. Carol Hegel, left, IFB Women's Committee chair, provided additional information to a teacher at the conclusion of the workshop.

The IFB Women's Committee conducted seminars several times each day at the 1982 Farm Progress Show's Farm Bureau exhibit tent near Wolcott. Featured was the new "Farming the Classroom" program. Games, prizes and general agricultural information were presented. Talking to the crowd is Carol Hegel, IFB women's committee chair.

tural products. These products included flour, meal, meat, and processed foods. At that time, these kinds of products accounted for one-third of U.S. agricultural exports. Increasing those sales would stimulate domestic economic activity and provide farmers and those involved in the value-added processing more income. Because of the many steps involved in producing these products, the more highly processed they are, the more economic activity is generated.

The farm organizations were successful in their mission. Secretary of Agriculture John Block recommended that the Foreign Agricultural Service supplement the available information on these products and to be alert for new economic opportunities that arose.

Around the same time, Marion Stackhouse spoke to a U. S. subcommittee on domestic monetary policy at a hearing in Indianapolis. He was critical of Congress for failing to fund the Commodity Credit Corporation Revolving Fund for fiscal 1982. The fund had been created to give low interest loans to foreign buyers desiring to buy American agricultural commodities. Without this fund, foreign buyers had to go through the Export-Import Bank and pay higher interest rates.

Furthermore, he told the subcommittee, the Farm Home Administration funds should be returned to their original purpose of assisting only farmers, rather than other businesses, which were more appropriately served by the Small Business Administration. He explained that many young farmers especially were suffering financially because of unwise farm monetary policies. Overall, the number of farm foreclosures was going up, with farmers both voluntarily and involuntarily turning their farms over to the FmHA.

The IFB urged President Ronald Reagan and Congress to bring down the deficit to reduce inflation and to take other measures to improve the economy as a whole, which would help the many farmers who found themselves in desperate financial conditions.

The 1982 Indiana harvest of corn, wheat, soybeans, oats, and hay was part of a record-high national yield. In Indiana's case, its portion of this harvest was accomplished on 3 million less acres than the previous year. Unfortunately, though, farmers had little reason to celebrate. The grain market was in poor financial shape, and overall national farm income was down 24 percent. The IFB tendered several proposals to the government to create a more favorable grain marketing atmosphere:

> 1) Increase export credit sales by: funding Commodity Credit Corporation revolving fund for export financing; renew Export Import Bank financing to farm commodities, and increase the use of Public Law 480 (food for peace) programs and initiate barter transactions.

> 2) Use government funds, if necessary, for export credit subsidies—either interest "buy down" or to meet the competition of European Communities subsidized commodity prices.

> 3) Paid land diversion program for 1983 crops.

> 4) Maintain present loan rates and target prices. (*The Hoosier Farmer*, November 1982.)

Along with these suggestions, the IFB encouraged the passage of legislation "to ensure the sanctity of contracts so that the United States will again be viewed as a reliable supplier in international trade."

By the end of 1982, the world economy was deeply entrenched in the worst recession in a quarter-century. The high living of the 1970s came to a halt, which meant that many countries, particularly developing nations, had high debts, preventing them from buying American agricultural products. These countries could not get the loans they needed to purchase food products. American farmers suffered greatly from the loss of this market.

Improving this situation would take a global effort, and improvement wouldn't happen quickly. In his presentation to the 1982 IFB convention delegates, Stackhouse offered his view of the situation:

> We are currently paying for many of the mistakes of the past. When we studied our high school physics, we learned that there is always a reaction to every action, and so I guess we should not have been too surprised to finally see this phenomenon bear down on us.
>
> When we have produced and consumed resources without concern for the future or for efficiency, we realize that this must come to an end. We found business expansion and costly services coming to us that we never wanted nor could afford because, in many cases, they were foisted upon us by industry and government. To be conservative in our spending, thoughts and expectations is not all bad. Whether we like it or not, this will be the mode for the coming years.

Once again, he urged the government "to stop using food to threaten other countries" and instead to use it "for the encouragement of other countries to follow in our footsteps of productivity and hard work." At the same time, he reminded delegates that the Farm Bureau had an important role to play in economic recovery as well in as the direction that the United States was to take. He urged members to educate themselves on the issues and to take a stand by voting on those issues. What Stackhouse called "the productive power of agriculture and the technology which is used in the research of agriculture" was crucial to the well-being of the country in many ways, offering a source of power for the people. He urged farmers to use not only the food they produced but their compassion and understanding to help clear up "the dark clouds on the horizon."

As in other times, farmers were being unfairly blamed for many of the economic problems the country faced in the early 1980s. As food costs rose due to inflation and other reasons, most people blamed the farmer, who had no ultimate control over the food processing costs and government policies and regulations that drove all costs up. In *The Hoosier Farmer* of February 1983, Stackhouse shared with his readers "A Farmer's Prayer" that he had received at Christmas. It summed up the feelings of many farmers:

> *Dear God, give us patience and wisdom to understand why a pound of steak at $1.89 is high, but a 3-ounce cocktail at $1.50 is okay, and Lord, help me to understand why $3.00 for a movie is not bad, but $3.50 for a bushel of wheat that makes 50 loaves of bread is unreasonable; a 50-cent coke at the ballgame is okay, but a 30-cent glass of milk is inflationary. Cotton is too high at 65 cents a pound, but a $2.00 shirt is a bargain. Corn is too steep at 3-cents worth in a box of flakes, but the flakes are sold for 50 cents per serving. While you are at it, dear God, please help me understand the consumer who drives by my field and raises his eyebrows when he sees me driving a $30,000 tractor that he helped put together so he could make money and drive down that right-of-way they took from me to build a road so he could go hunting. Thank you, God, for your past guidance. I hope you can help me make some sense out of all this and please, God, send some rain.*

Donald Henderson, left, director, IFB National Affairs Department, talks with U.S. Congressman Bud Hillis. Henderson was in Washington, D.C., and appeared before the House Agriculture committee to discuss portions of the farm program dealing with wheat, soybeans and feed grains under the 1985 Farm Bill.

Chapter Six

PACs, Checkoffs, and Legislation

Even though the 1980s were tough on agriculture, the various organizations affiliated with the IFB forged ahead, as they always did. The Producers Marketing Association scored a national first in November 1982. At 1 p.m. on that day, it sold slaughter cattle by computer—the first time in the country for a computerized sale of this kind by any organization. As Gene Shaver, PMA general manager, wrote in the January 1983 issue of *The Hoosier Farmer*, "PMA entered five loads of slaughter cattle into the computer and actually offered to sell to the highest bidder the listed cattle while they were still at their feed bunks at home." All the cattle were sold in 10 minutes. This was the beginning of a regularly scheduled weekly sale via computer. Direct feed lot and telephone sales continued.

The computer selling preserved the central market auction that the PMA had always employed. All buyers had equal opportunity to bid, and interested buyers had a chance to see the cattle before making their bids. Buyers could purchase cattle from any location that had a phone and an electrical outlet since the computers were easily transportable.

Lambs were also being sold electronically, although the first sales were held monthly because the lamb market was not as large as the cattle market. Later, the sales were increased to twice monthly. Because the individual lamb pools in the various states were so small, PMA joined with livestock organizations in other Midwestern states to create a larger pool.

One bright spot in the livestock business during this time was the increase in demand by foreign countries for American meat products and live animals. In 1981, 3.3 million tons of beef were exported, a 50 percent increase in the previous decade. *The Hoosier Farmer* reported that this area of livestock marketing "could prove to be a real growth potential over the next decade."

Congressional District 5 ELECT, IFB's political action committee, conducted a 1985 meeting and farm tour near Peru. Among attendees were from left: U.S. Congressman Bud Hillis; Don Henderson, IFB national affairs director; Larry Boys, Miami County FB president; and Steve Maple, Miami County FB vice president and ELECT trustee.

Despite the bad economy, the Indiana Farm Bureau Cooperative Association was also going strong in the early 1980s, with sales of $1.126 billion for fiscal year 1982. The message of the 1982 annual meeting of the IFBCA was, according to Philip French, executive vice president, that the "co-op can make a difference in helping farmers cope with today's economic crisis and, of equal importance, helping farmers to take advantage of tomorrow's opportunities."

Long accustomed to raising its voice to make sure that farmers' concerns were heard in the political and legislative matters at the state and federal level, the IFB took a significant political step in 1983 when it established a political action committee, or PAC. Don Henderson, who was director of the National Affairs Department, was named secretary of the PAC, which was called Indiana Farm Bureau ELECT.

The PAC system was created by Congress in 1972 as a way to encourage more individuals to contribute to candidates they wished to see elected. PACs would collect funds from members and then make a group contribution to chosen candidates.

A large part of the reason why the IFB formed the PAC, in Don Henderson's words years later, was because Marion Stackhouse, who was president of the organization at this time, was "a visionary. He was one of the few people that I've known in my lifetime who had the ability to look 10 years ahead and see pretty clearly what was coming. He saw agriculture and other industries as being much more regulated, that the regulatory side of government was going to play a lot larger role in our business. And he felt that we needed a physical presence in Washington for our organization."

Looking back to the beginnings of PAC in Indiana, Harry Pearson recalled, "I can remember, I was plowing on the farm where I was born. I was vice president at the time. Marion Stackhouse was coming back from a meeting. He climbed up in the tractor with me and we plowed a couple of rounds together. He talked about the PAC and asked my opinion on its practicality and benefits for Indiana farmers.

"I'm sure he did this with most or all of the district directors to get their comments and ideas which helped him and others formulate the concept and eventual plan that was presented to the board by Henderson."

Governor Robert Orr proclaimed March 21 as "Indiana Ag Day 1983." Joining the ceremony were from left: Gary Swaim, Indiana division of agriculture director; Judy Carley, IFB Women's Division & Ag Day committee secretary; Lt. Gov. John Mutz, Indiana commissioner of agriculture; Max Crowder, Elanco & Ag Day committee vice chair; Gary Geswein, Indiana Young Farmers & Ag Day committee chair; and Tom Asher, IFB Information & Public Relations Division and Ag Day committee treasurer. Indiana Ag Day recognized the importance of the Hoosier farmer and agriculture to Indiana's economy.

Ross Riggs, left, general manager, Indiana Agricultural Marketing Association, waits on another buyer of IAMA goods at the 1983 state convention. Available products included cheese varieties, popcorn, peanuts, and pecans.

So Henderson took the idea of an IFB PAC to the board of directors, who asked that he conduct a poll among the counties. He chose several counties in various congressional districts, both urban and rural, in the north and south of the state. The poll came back in favor of forming a PAC.

In an interview with *The Hoosier Farmer* in October 1983, Henderson added another reason why the IFB should have a PAC. "I am very concerned that in the future Farm Bureau's legislative program will not be as effective unless we become more involved in the political process of electing qualified candidates," he said. "Today, our farm votes alone will not elect good farm candidates because we, as farmers, are only approximately 2.5% of the population."

The only way to help get candidates who supported farm positions into office, he concluded, was to help them get elected. And the only way the IFB could do that in a legal manner was through a PAC. Any IFB member could join simply by contributing $1 to the PAC.

As with other IFB decisions, the PAC was arranged on a county level. Each county Farm Bureau had two representatives called trustees who served on a congressional district-wide committee to evaluate and determine the candidates that ELECT would support. Those candidates would actually be endorsed only if two-thirds of the trustees in the district committee voted to endorse them. No state officer, director, or staff person had any vote in who would be endorsed.

If the county Farm Bureaus did not support the PAC effort, it would not succeed—which is the way it should be, said Henderson.

He believed that the creation of a PAC, even though the IFB had never endorsed candidates in the past, was not a drastic change in philosophy. In the interview, he stated, "I believe we are seeing a willingness of our leadership and our membership to use an additional tool in our legislative effort."

By late 1984, counties in four congressional districts had joined the PAC, with members contributing about $10,000. As Marion Stackhouse told the 1984 IFB convention,

> The counties which were involved this year did an outstanding job in evaluating and analyzing the congressmen's contributions to agriculture. We think the congressional people appreciate our concern, interest, and support, and four contributions were made to the candidates who held that office. All four of these people were re-elected, and will no doubt, have a better feeling for how farmers view issues as a result of our concern and interest in their political careers. (*The Hoosier Farmer*, January 1985)

Thus, with its first election, the PAC was off to an excellent start.

In the two years previous to 1984, Indiana's population had dropped by an estimated 28,000. Yet IFB membership had grown to nearly 260,000. This

Harrison County Farm Bureau's first annual agricultural career expo was held at the Corydon High School. A few of the many people responsible for the success of the career day were from left: Jerry Couch, IFB fieldman, Shelby Willis, expo chairman; Don Jones, Harrison County FB president; Scott McKain, WHAS-TV personality and guest speaker; and Randall Walker, IFB district 10 director.

The Indiana State Police and Indiana Farm Bureau started a marijuana eradication program in 1984. Participating in the media conference kicking off the campaign were from left: Prentice White, Drug Enforcement Administration special agent; John Shettle, state police superintendent; Indiana Governor Robert Orr; IFB President Marion Stackhouse; and Lt. Larry Delaney, state police commander at the Lowell district.

number included a growing number of farmer-members, despite the shrinking number of farmers in Indiana.

There was also some good news on the economic front. Food prices went up only 2.1 percent—the smallest amount of any year in the previous 16. Unfortunately, the farm price share of food declined by 2.2 percent. Most of that decline was due to lower prices for meat animals and fresh fruit. According to *The Hoosier Farmer* of July 1984,

> Once again, it is the farmers' tremendous ability to produce that created surplus situations that when coupled with decreasing export demands helped the consumer.
> But for the farmer, this along with high interest rates continued to exert tremendous pressures on the survivability of many in production agriculture.

A milestone for Farm Bureau Insurance occurred during 1984: On October 17, the company marked the beginning of its 50th year. At a Charter Day celebration in Indianapolis, Marion Stackhouse, president of the insurance company, and John O. Hutchins, chief executive officer, were presented with a replica of the company's original charter by Lt. Gov. John Mutz and Commissioner of Insurance Don Miller. This was the beginning of a year-long celebration.

The insurance company had experienced a very successful half-century of operation. After its first year of operation in 1935, it showed a surplus of $148.01 and 5000 policyholders. Year-end figures from 1983 showed combined capital and surplus of more than $104 million and nearly 1 million policyholders.

October 17, 1984 marked the beginning of the 50th year of Farm Bureau Insurance. To honor the occasion, state officials presented Farm Bureau with a replica of the company's original charter. From left are: Executive Vice President John Hutchins, Farm Bureau Insurance companies; Marion Stackhouse, IFB president; Indiana's Lt. Gov. John Mutz; Edwin Simcox, Indiana secretary of state; and Don Miller, insurance commissioner.

The home office staff in 1984 numbered 750, and more than 600 agents and 250 claims personnel rounded out the total complement of Farm Bureau Insurance employees, distributed among 118 sales offices and eight regional

United Farm Bureau Family Life Insurance became a $2 billion company when its life insurance in force totaled $2,015,333,314. Executive Vice President Jack Rosebrough, right, made the announcement October 12, 1977. Helping celebrate with the traditional cake in the home office was Marion Stackhouse, IFB president.

claims offices. During the fiftieth-year celebrations, the company rededicated itself to its original goal of providing the "best possible insurance and the lowest possible cost."

The Hoosier Farmer remarked, "Much of the companies success can be attributed to mutual trust between policy holders and agents, as well as trust between policyholders and claims representatives."

Other celebratory events were planned throughout the coming year: License Day celebration on February 26, 1985; a parade of 1935 model cars; and a dinner party for agents, employees, and retirees of the company in October 1985.

The life insurance company reached a milestone in April when it crossed the $4 billion mark of policies in force. The life company had reached the billion-dollar mark in 1972, and then hit $2 billion five years later. That number was doubled to $4 billion in 1985—only seven years later. This accomplishment was announced to more than 300 agents at the Trailblazer Banquet in Las Vegas, Nevada, in mid-April. The $4 billion figure represented 174,824 policies in the Farm Bureau Insurance companies.

During 1984 the IFB offered specially designed computer systems, through its Farm Records Service Company, to farmer-members who wanted to track various aspects of their operations by computer. Hayden King, computer sales manager, was in charge of this program.

The package included the computer with choice of printers, a complete software package, and programs to cover every aspect of a farming operation, including financial accounting and check writing.

At the beginning of the year, about 700 members were keeping their records on a farm record keeping system, which was being updated to accept electronic transmissions from those farmers with home computers. Included in the program were resource management, crop and livestock profitability planning, enterprise analysis, complete training for those using the system, equipment set-up, and the establishment of a Farm Bureau user group.

On another technology front was Farm Bureau's coal experiment. The agricultural economy was depressed during the mid-1980s when Farm Bureau learned of a laboratory process that removed sulfur from coal.

Farm Bureau Insurance became a $4 billion dollar company in 1985. Reviewing the printout showing $4,016, 836,662 worth of life insurance in force were from left: Hugo Anderson, senior vice president, marketing; Tom Ulmer, executive vice president; and Roy Dittman, senior vice president, United Farm Bureau Life Insurance Company. In 1972, the Life Company surpassed $1 billion. President of the Insurance companies was Marion Stackhouse.

Many areas of southern Indiana contained sulfur-rich coal deposits. High sulfur forces power generating plants to install expensive scrubbers to remove the element before it reaches the atmosphere. The organization felt that if the process could be adapted to a commercial scale there would be several benefits. With energy prices rising, this could provide a reasonably-priced energy source for electric generation. It could help those farmers in southern Indiana who had coal deposits under their land. And it would boost the economy of Indiana.

UFB Development was formed in 1984 to fund Midwest Ore Partnership. An alliance was formed with Pure Fuels, Nevada, and an agreement was signed with Black Beauty Coal Company in Indiana.

A facility was built in 1985 to test the process proven successful by two independent laboratories. The prototype design and commercial results were unsuccessful. The project was abandoned in 1990. UFB did retain the royalty rights on the process for 50 years or until 2040.

Around this same time, Congress announced plans to remove a prohibition on a less technological kind of work that had long been done at home by women. The Fair Labor Standards Act of 1943 prohibited the home manufacture of knitted outerware for sale, but a push was underway 40 years later to remove this clause from the FLSA. Labor organizations opposed this change in the law, yet the IFB and other groups interested in home employment met with the Secretary of Labor to urge his support for the change.

Originally implemented to prevent the creation of sweatshop-type operations, the law also prohibited farm women from earning extra income by making knitted outerwear garments for sale. These women were among the most ardent supporters of removal of the prohibition. Carol Hegel, chair of the IFB Women's Committee, urged Indiana farm women to contact their senators to support amendment of the bill. As *The Hoosier Farmer* of May 1984 reported,

> The Indiana Farm Bureau women point out that computers are creating a new center of productivity in the home for thousands of Americans seeking more income. Yet, persons with an equally valuable skill, such as the making of ladies' clothing, are denied the right to earn an income doing this at home because of U.S. Department of Labor regulations...
>
> Mrs. Hegel says, "We must plan with an eye on the future and encourage productivity where technology and the time dictate. Many farm women are looking for ways to earn extra money working at home, so this is important to them.

One "golden" spot during 1984 was the promotion of Indiana soybeans, called "the 'gold' that grows" in numerous issues of *The Hoosier Farmer* that year. Grown in many states, soybeans are an important crop in Indiana, and one that in the mid-1980s was quickly growing in export value.

U.S. Senator Richard Lugar, second from left, was presented with a plaque from the American Soybean Association in 1983 citing his efforts in sponsoring the contract sanctity bill in the U. S. Congress. Among the ag group supporters was Farm Bureau. Making the presentation were from left: Bill Silver, Indiana Soybean Growers Association president; Lugar; B.B. Spratling, American Soybean Association president; and Joe Pearson, American Soybean Association director from Indiana.

The IFB, the Indiana Soybean Growers Association, and their members joined with other farmers and their organizations in 23 states to create a national soybean checkoff program. Already in use for other agricultural products, the checkoff program was an effective way for growers of a commodity to organize as a group to promote their products—for only 1 cent per bushel. According to an ad from the Indiana Soybean Growers Association in *The Hoosier Farmer*, this penny would help "unlock demand for soybeans, worldwide soybean sales, returns from research, new uses for soybeans, (and) favorable trade policies."

In 1983, 60 percent of the American soybean crop was sold overseas in a variety of forms and for a variety of uses. Included in these uses, according to *The Hoosier Farmer*,

> Farmers feed U. S. soybean meal to pigs in the Dominican Republic, poultry in Pakistan and dairy cows in Japan. Bakers in Paris add soybean flour to their breads. And consumers in the United Kingdom are learning that their favorite margarines and cooking oil are made with soybean oil. (March 1984)

Indiana Farm Bureau promoted a "Yes" vote in the 1984 soybean referendum. Indiana was one of the few states without a self-help program designed to increase market demand. Some 10,000 producers needed to register to assure a vote in the check-off program. Promoting a "yes" for soybeans were Joe and Forrest Ferguson, Dupont.

The reason these people became interested in using soybean products in the first place was

> Because U. S. farmers know that if they don't sell their own soybeans, no one else is going to do it for them. So through a program called the soybean checkoff, U. S. farmers sponsor seminars, conferences, trade fairs, feeding trials, product promotion, literature translations and trade team travel. (March 1984)

The Hoosier Farmer ran articles all year discussing the soybean and its current and potential markets and uses. The IFB encouraged soybean farmers to say "yes for soybeans" and participate in the referendum on the Soybean Market Development and Research Program that was scheduled for the coming January. As Don Villwock, a soybean farmer from Southern Indiana who would be elected IFB vice president at the 1998 state convention, wrote,

> We must compete and show our customers that we have the preferred product. In the depressed agriculture market today, we can ill afford to lose any new or traditional markets. Isn't it only right that those who have the most to lose should lead the fight to keep our markets? If the Indiana soybean farmer who exports over 60% of his beans doesn't care, who will?

The soybean checkoff finally passed on the third attempt, and a program began in 1991, with farmers investing one-half of one percent of the net market value of their soybeans. A referendum in 1994 reaffirming the checkoff passed nationwide.

In 1987, the Indiana General Assembly passed legislation that established guidelines by which Hoosier corn farmers could establish a corn check-off in their state. The IFB supported the check-off. Signed into law on June 2, this legislation called for corn producers to vote for an assessment of a half-cent per bushel, which would be automatically checked-off at the time of sale. As with soybeans, the money raised would be directed toward maintaining and creating markets for Hoosier corn, along with research of new uses and market education.

During the corn checkoff campaign, the Indiana Corn Growers Association educated farmers on some of the reasons it was important to vote for the program. They stressed the research aspect, since developing new uses for farm products would continue to expand markets. Some of the existing or potential uses for corn were intriguing. For instance, corn could be used in the manufacture of biodegradable plastics, a cornstarch-based road de-icer, and, amazingly, coal desulfurization, which was important in Indiana because most of the coal mined there had a high sulfur content (mixing high-sulfur coal and ethanol, which was made from corn, ties up the sulfur, and the coal then meets EPA clean-air standards). Other uses for corn could be found in starch-based chemicals, medical applicants, textiles, and cornstarch by-product industrial applications.

The enabling legislation for the corn check-off, which was signed into law by Gov. Robert Orr, also called for a referendum conducted by the Commissioner of Agriculture's Office to be held among Indiana corn farmers, and also for the creation of a 15-member council to oversee administration of the funds. The program was predicted to generate $1.5 million to $2 million annually.

When the time came for the referendum, 55,000 ballots were mailed out, and 25,000 valid ballots were returned. Despite all the promotion of the check-off, Indiana corn farmers defeated it with a 62.9 percent "no" vote.

In 1988, Hoosier beef producers voted three-to-one for a beef checkoff program, which would give them a producer-controlled promotion and research programs. This made the Indiana beef industry the first major commodity in the state to pass a checkoff.

Pork producers followed suit in September 1988 when they, too, voted for a checkoff for their product. They were to pay 25¢ for each $100 when a hog was sold.

In 1985, the IFB turned a spotlight on the federal budget, which was severely out of balance with a rapidly growing deficit—"federal spending red ink (growing) to nightmarish proportions"—causing many adverse reactions throughout the economy, including agriculture. The IFB urged its members to contact their senators and representatives about bringing the federal budget in line with federal expenditures. It was crucial that they deliver this message because, as Stackhouse wrote,

> It has been easy for congress to spend your money for all the things that people ask for and, therefore, become popular and get re-elected. Deficit spending has gotten so far out of balance that to continue this course of action could jeopardize our ability to survive as a nation...
>
> All items must come under scrutiny of the budget including agriculture, but this does not mean that agriculture has to take a 50 percent cut while other segments receive money for all their pet projects. Even though most of our Indiana congressmen are on our side in this issue, they need your letters of support and strength if it is going to happen in Washington. (*The Hoosier Farmer*, May 1985)

Don Henderson, director of the IFB National Affairs Department, also urged members to emphasize budget issues with Congress. He wrote in his monthly column in *The Hoosier Farmer* that the IFB supported an amendment to the Constitution that would require the federal government to operate each year on a balanced budget. He added that a balanced budget should not be achieved through new or increased taxes. The IFB supported a joint resolution of the House and Senate that proposed such an amendment.

Farm Bureau's float in the 1984 Farmers Day Parade during the Indiana State Fair was an attractive, three-section original design depicting the theme-"The Hands that Feed Us."

Indiana Governor Robert Orr visited with District Woman Leader Shirley Woody, Lebanon, during 1985 Indiana Agriculture Day festivities at the Indianapolis City Market. To the right is Jeannette McCabe, Oxford, district woman leader.

In 1985, *The Hoosier Farmer* carried many articles on the federal budget so that IFB members would be well informed. One article in the May issue, from a senior economist of the American Farm Bureau Federation, recapped the reasons for the current budget problems and proposed some solutions:

Between 1970 and 1980, real (inflation adjusted) total federal revenues increased 37.5 percent and real total federal spending increased 54.8 percent. During the same period, real Gross National Product (GNP) increased 36.3 percent, about the same rate of growth as real federal receipts. Federal spending grew at a much faster rate than the private economy that had to carry the public sector burden. As a result, productivity growth declined and unemployment increased. Inflation increased rapidly as the Federal Reserve was leaned on to finance more and more transfer payment and benefit largesse from Congress...

Since 1978, Farm Bureau has called on Congress to reform entitlement laws in order to get control of spending. Farm Bureau advocates a "Freeze and Fix" approach to federal spending. "Freeze" total federal spending, except for interest payments, at the previous year's level of appropriations and keep the total frozen until Congress "fixes" the laws that cause the spending overruns.

Further, Farm Bureau favors examining all federal spending departments, agencies, and programs for spending cuts. Farm Bureau supports the line item veto authority for the President to whittle away at special interest spending. Farm Bureau supports a constitutional amendment to limit taxes and spending to a percentage of GNP.

The "freeze and fix" proposal also called for a period of three years during which all cost-of-living increases would be frozen.

In March 1985, 51 IFB leaders visited their legislators in Washington, D.C., to discuss the federal budget and interest rates, which were very high and going higher, much to the detriment of many farm operations. By coincidence, their visit came on the same day that President Ronald Reagan vetoed the additional credit bill for farmers.

Along with the congressional delay in passing a new farm bill, the deficit was causing a great deal of instability in the commodity markets, which was affecting farm credit. The IFB board of directors appointed a panel to investigate credit issues for farmers and then present some policy positions for the coming year. Members of the committee came from the banking industry, the farm credit system and Farmers Home Administration, Purdue University, the lieutenant governor's office, and agriculture.

Some 250 Hoosier farmers in 50 counties donated close to 2,000 tons of hay to drought stricken South & North Carolina, Georgia and Virginia farmers in 1986. Johnson County farmers contributed 1,200 bales, which were delivered to Johnson County fairgrounds near Franklin. In Georgia an estimated 60-80 percent overall crop loss and a nearly complete loss of pasture and hay was reported.

The creation of this committee was not meant to "push the panic button," according to Stackhouse, but simply to get "our thoughts in line and our positions ready" in case of an emergency. Along with other IFB members and members of the American Farm Bureau Federation, Stackhouse believed that the time had come for farmers, banks, the farm credit system, and the government to pool their ideas to arrive at a solid solution to the country's, and agriculture's, financial challenges of the day. He reminded all IFB members that their suggestions were very much appreciated.

The country's financial situation in the mid-1980s caused a great deal of hardship for many farmers, some of whom lost their farms due to heavy debt (although half of all farmers remained solvent). The public attitude toward farmers shifted as their plight became known. The Farm Aid concert, presented by musician Willie Nelson and others, attempted to raise $50 million dollars to help struggling farmers; the final tally was actually much less, perhaps $10 million, but it brought to the public an increased awareness of the challenges that farmers faced on a daily basis. Support for farmers increased so much that one poll revealed that 55 percent of the American public would be willing to pay more taxes to help troubled farmers save their land.

During these lean times, the number of farm families who required or desired income from non-farm sources grew quickly. A 1987 survey showed that 20 percent of gross income for Indiana farm families came from non-farm sources. At that same time, nearly half the farm women in the United States worked away from home, either part-time or full-time. This kind of transition was very difficult for many families since the women usually handled the many household responsibilities along with farm tasks. In order to assist families with this change, the IFB State Women's Committee created a program called "The New You." They were assisted by Career Consultants of Indianapolis and received funding from the Indiana Office of Occupational Development.

The program was designed to help farm women and their families make the best transition possible and to "provide the educational, motivational, and realistic base to become 'The New You.'" The committee asked women who had taken a job off the farm, or who were preparing to do so, to share their experiences so that other families might benefit. They also provided a form that women could complete to tell the committee the kinds of information and services they most desired from The New You program.

Other farm women and men began their own businesses at home as a way to obtain additional income. Many of these women began asking their extension agents for help and information with these ventures, so Purdue University Cooperative Extension created a program called "Beginning Business."

The Extension offices began holding county and area seminars. Among the topics covered were assessing skills before starting a business, obtaining financing, legal information, and establishing prices.

An estimated 300,000 attended the 1985 Farm Progress Show near Knightstown. Carol Hegel, center, handed out materials and encouraged visitors to learn more about Farm Bureau's activities. Displays emphasized tax and record keeping services, AgriVisor and educational programs.

The Extension Service created a video tape on starting a home-based business and loaned it for home use. It covered many of the same topics as the seminars. With the help of business professionals, the Extension Service also produced several pamphlets on various aspects of running a small business. Those individuals who ran sewing businesses out of their homes could subscribe to a new newsletter called "Sew What?"

The program was very successful, with more than 150 people taking advantage of it during the first six months. Judith Carley, director of the IFB Women's Department, was coordinator of the program. She said The New You helped these individuals think through their skills and assets. The various activities were designed to help participants to set goals and priorities, as well as how to implement them.

Some people who attended the Beginning Business events decided they didn't want to open a home-based business after all, but this was also beneficial because they saved time and money by not starting up and then having to close the business later.

In 1985, the IFB continued its interest in state government and issues. In that year, the organization was concerned about proper highway financing and higher utility rates, both of which, while not strictly farm-related issues, would have an affect on farm families. Stackhouse was asked to serve on the board of directors of Public Service Indiana, one of the state's utility companies, as a voice for the state's agricultural sector. He accepted this responsibility, writing in *The Hoosier Farmer*,

> I feel Indiana Farm Bureau is honored by my being asked to serve on the PSI Board of Directors. I can assure you that I will do my best to bring the farmers' viewpoint to an industry that needs your help. Farmers have invested a lot of money in bringing electricity to their farms, and now is not the time to avoid facing the problems. It will take some time, but there will be brighter days ahead for farmers and the utility industry. (June 1985)

Later, as when dealing with energy issues as a member of the Hoosiers for Economic Development Committee, Stackhouse suggested that the council investigate the time it took to build a new coal-fired generating plant, which in the mid-1980s was 8 to 10 years. One step he recommended was for government inspectors take a more helpful stance and offer direction during the planning and building processes, rather than by acting as adversaries searching out areas of non-compliance after the fact. He also believed that streamlining the regulatory process would help shorten the time span—which would reduce the cost to the utility building the plant as well as to the customers who would eventually bear the costs.

In January 1986, Gene Shaver retired as general manager of the Producers Marketing Association. He first came to the organization in 1970 from the Interstate Producers Livestock Association to head the PMA. He had been asked to lead the organization at a time of great financial difficulty.

Although he was confident he could help the PMA get back on its feet, he nevertheless had some concerns about taking over the reins at that time. Many years after his retirement he recalled, "You can imagine the morale of the employees. Here is the company they've worked all their lives for and with, and it was totally destroyed. They didn't know if they had a job or could rebuild it, or what. So it took a considerable amount of hand holding and encouragement. So it was a matter of saying, 'Look, fellows, we got a job to do. Let's do it. You know how.'"

U.S. Senator Dan Quayle, right, greeted reporters at the Stackhouse farm near Westfield. Marion Stackhouse (arms folded), IFB president, listens as Quayle acknowledges the endorsement for his re-election to the U.S. Senate by IFB's ELECT political action committee trustees. According to Stackhouse, "Quayle had a 92 percent "yes" record on key votes for farmers, the highest percentage of any Indiana legislator in Washington.

Shaver was grateful for the support of the IFB leadership when he came on board. "The work climate for me as manager was excellent," he said. "The Farm Bureau board was understanding. They're patient, they're kind. They know the marketing business pretty well."

That he did his job well for 15 years was evident in a retirement tribute from Marion Stackhouse:

> He brought confidence to the organization at that time, and has constantly worked to bring PMA back to its present net worth. Gene also restored confidence to the customer, the market and the employees by his honesty, forthrightness and integrity....
>
> As you see Gene from time to time in his life of retirement, give him a warm handshake and thank him for all the good work he has done. May his life encourage others to give their best for the good of Indiana agriculture. (*The Hoosier Farmer*, March 1986.)

In September 1987, the IFB suffered the loss of another respected leader. Marion Stackhouse died from a heart attack on September 6 at home on his Westfield farm. He was 64.

He had served the IFB for 35 years, beginning as a field representative in 1950. He became director of the Commodity Department in 1960, and in 1976 he was elected president. During his tenure, he served as president of the Farm Bureau Mutual Insurance Company of Indiana, the United Farm Bureau Life Insurance Company, Producers Marketing Association Inc., the Indiana Agricultural Marketing Association, and the Indiana Farm Bureau Service Company. He was also a member of the executive committee and board of directors of the American Farm Bureau Federation, and director-at-large of the IFBCA.

In addition to his service on Farm Bureau-related organizations, Stackhouse had been appointed by U.S. Secretary of Agriculture Richard Lyng to the Federal Grain Inspection Service Advisory Committee and was in his second two-year term when he died. He also served on the Office of Technology Assessment's advisory panel to enhance grain quality in international trade and was chairman of the Indiana Highway Users Conference and a director of the Highway Users Federation.

Shortly after Stackhouse's death, Doug Nagel, a member of the State Young Farmer Committee, suggested a fitting tribute to this great IFB leader: "I would encourage anyone, whose life Marion touched, to give a never-ending memorial by working together to make Farm Bureau stronger and better than ever before." (*The Hoosier Farmer*, September 25, 1987)

The IFB board of directors visited former Indiana Governor Otis Bowen, M.D, and current (July 1987) Office of Health & Human Services secretary, Washington, D.C. First row from left: Harry Pearson, vice president; Carol Hegel, second vice president; Bowen; Marion Stackhouse, president; and Harold Luck, D3. Standing from left: Darlton Lavengood, D4; Marvin Metzger, corporate secretary; Ralph Ponsler, D8; Mary Ferris, D6; Mike Zimmerman, D2; Conrad Begeman, D7; Don Henderson, national affairs department; Howard Rippy, D5; Randall Walker, D10; Wayne Emigh, D1; and Robert Harper, D9.

Harry Pearson, a partner in the family farm operation in Blackford County, was first elected president in 1987.

Harry Pearson, who was vice president of the IFB at the time of Stackhouse's death, was appointed acting president until the December convention. He wrote a touching tribute to the man who had been a positive example of leadership for him:

I have had the opportunity to work with many people in agriculture during the last 30 years, but none have I admired more than Marion Stackhouse. He was a diamond in the rough. Working close to him as vice president during the past 5 years provided me with a perspective of him at work that many did not have the opportunity to see. He was always thinking and had the ability to see the "big picture," and to know where the pieces all fit. He understood in a real way those farmers who were struggling financially to stay in business, and worked tirelessly on their behalf. He was firm, but always fair and compassionate in dealing with others, yet he had time to keep his priorities of God, family, and his work in proper order. (*The Hoosier Farmer*, Oct. 23, 1987)

Two candidates for the presidential vacancy emerged: Don Henderson, IFB national affairs director, and Pearson. Both men had excellent qualifications for the post, and it was up to the convention delegates to decide between them. They chose Pearson and then elected Henderson as vice president. He edged out vice president hopefuls Carolyn Hegel, second vice president and chair of the State Women's Committee, and Randall Walker, District 10 director.

With Pearson at the helm, the IFB continued its tradition of informing, educating, and assisting Indiana farmers. Among his first tasks as president, he led IFB voting delegates at the AFBF convention in January 1988 to help pass a national resolution that opposed federal legislation that would allow public access to or through private property without the owner's permission.

At the state level during this time, the IFB was mostly successful in its work with the General Assembly—a process in which the county state legislative coordinators were very active. Among the successes that benefitted Indiana farmers: funding for a new Animal Disease Diagnostic Laboratory at Purdue University; a farm mediation bill for farmers and their lenders; a new law that added sheep and wool to the list of commodities that producers can petition for a referendum and a checkoff; reinstatement of the Egg Board and

Indiana Farm Bureau's legislative team in 1986 was: (l. to r.) Owen Mohler, Bill Marvel, Meredith Kincaid, and Bill Hadley. Farm Bureau issues during the general assembly included seed laws, elevator bankruptcy, changes to the local option tax law, and restricting the transfer of interest monies generated by investments from the school cumulative building funds to the general fund.

the Creamery Licensing, which had been scheduled for "sunsetting"; a guaranteed loan fund for various diversified agriculture products; and a blocking of the proposal to delay property tax assessment from 1990 to 1991.

By June, many Indiana farmers had little to celebrate. A serious drought that covered most of the country, combined with below normal subsoil moisture conditions, was beginning to affect their crops. Low rainfall continued through the summer, and farmers worried about their livelihoods. As Harry Pearson wrote in *The Hoosier Farmer*,

> Rain —that precious God-given commodity. How quickly our thoughts have turned from a talked-about wet spring to one of the driest (early) summers in history. Farmers are no longer thinking of another good year to help them on the road to recovery. Instead, thoughts are now on dry pastures, hay shortages, reduced yields, inactivated chemicals, changed marketing strategies, margin calls, cash flows that may not work, plus many other related problems. Much of the debt restructuring of many farmers that was just beginning to work is once again in jeopardy. (June 24, 1988)

The drought threatened to have a big effect on national farm policy, but the IFB and sister Farm Bureau organizations called on the federal government to leave the provisions of the 1985 Food and Security Act, or farm bill, in place, saying it was working to move farm prices back to the market system. They urged Congress not to take hasty steps that could cause more devastation in the long run than the drought. Don Henderson also recommended staying the course, saying, "Our challenge today, as farmers, is to resist the temptation to allow government to move us away from the 1985 Farm Bill." He lauded Secretary of Agriculture Richard Lyng for taking prudent, rather than hasty, action in assessing farmers' needs and providing assistance to those farmers who needed it.

The drought caused a rapid drop in agricultural stockpiles, and the IFB recommended that the government not impose another embargo to keep stocks from dropping further. As Henderson wrote in the July 8, 1988, edition of *The Hoosier Farmer*,

> If we are to be reliable suppliers and be respected for selling quality products, embargoes, for any reason, are not in our short-term or long-term interests...We need to be very careful that the effects of record breaking dry weather is not used by marketplace opponents to derail our return to supply-demand economics.

The drought continued through the summer, and the IFB polled farmers across the state to see how they were faring. By mid-July, at least 50 percent of the Indiana corn crop was lost, with some counties suffering a 75 percent loss. Another concern was pastures and livestock feed, with many Hoosier pastures being completely destroyed by lack of rain. Since hay was also in short supply, many Indiana livestock producers had no inexpensive or nearby source of that product. Fruit and vegetables also suffered, with at least half the crops being lost. At the time of the survey, soybeans and tobacco losses were not yet known, although some soybean farmers feared the loss of half their crop.

One question on the survey, which was taken among 260 farmers across all of Indiana's 92 counties, was, "Is there anything specific relating to the drought that Farm Bureau should be doing on behalf of farmers?" The number one suggestion was "Pray for rain."

The IFB made other contributions by publishing a variety of drought-related articles throughout the summer in *The Hoosier Farmer*. Among the topics covered were the USDA/Congressional Drought Task Force meetings; crop insurance, milk production, and fertilizer options during a drought, emergency forage crops, feed alternatives, consumers and food prices, and the depression the drought situation might cause in farm families.

Purdue University School of Agriculture set up a drought hotline, which farmers could call for answers to a variety of drought-related questions, including where to find hay, how to battle spider mites that had infested dried-out soybean fields, and what to feed livestock. Established by the university's Drought Response Team, it was staffed by dozens of agricultural specialists from the Ag School and the Cooperative Extension Service, who answered more than 2,500 calls in the first three weeks. Secretary of Agriculture Lyng visited the campus in July to obtain input on upcoming drought-relief legislation and to take a first-hand look at Hoosier farms. By this time, Indiana's drought-ravaged corn crop had been rated as the worst in the nation.

The Drought Response Team offered other services to Indiana farmers: a drought summary, with the latest news on crop conditions, livestock problems, etc.; weekly televised briefings by Purdue agriculture specialists; agriculture economic outlook programs; a computerized national forage locator; and the reactivation of the Family and Agricultural Resource Management Program, which offered financial counseling to farmers. Pearson later praised the team's work as "second to none to that provided by anyone else throughout the country."

State Farm Bureau presidents, including Harry Pearson, gathered in Washington, D.C., in mid-July for a briefing on the drought crisis at the White House. President Ronald Reagan promised to do everything he could to protect farmers from excessive losses related to the dry weather.

On his return to Indianapolis, Pearson reported that the President was indeed truly concerned and was taking a prudent approach to the situation. For instance, he said that no relief program should require farmers to plow under their crops and that drought relief does not harm the benefits gained from the 1985 farm bill. The next month, Congress approved up to $6.8 billion in aid to farmers across the country affected by the drought.

In April 1986, the Indiana Farm Bureau board of directors were: (l. to r.) Merrill Ferris, D6; Ralph Ponsler, D8; Randall Walker, D10; Harold Luck, D3; Darlton Lavengood, D4; Harry Pearson, IFB vice president; Wayne Emigh, D1; Harold Myers, D2; Marion Stackhouse, IFB president; Howard Rippy, D5; Carol Hegel, IFB second vice president; Robert Harper, D9; and Conrad Begeman, D7.

The situation became so bad that the temptation was strong among many desperate farmers to be more concerned about quickly-applied, short-term aid measures, rather than the long-term view. This could lead to many more problems in terms of national farm policy when the drought was over. To avoid that kind of scenario, Pearson reminded Indiana farmers that they should not sacrifice their long-standing beliefs during this difficult time. In the August 5, 1988, issue of *The Hoosier Farmer*, he wrote,

> The drought of recent weeks has made us (farmers) painfully aware of the devastating losses many farmers are facing again, but can ill afford, following the greatest financial readjustment in agriculture since the 1930s.
>
> There is no question that some financial assistance to affected farmers is needed, and is necessary to prevent the rippling effect that will occur through the entire agricultural sector.
>
> However, the attitude of many farmers, or those representing them today, should be of great concern to all of us. We're all climbing on the "hand-out" wagon, whether always needed or not. Everyone is talking equity—and equity today means, "I want my share," not just help for those who truly need it.
>
> There are legitimate times when farmers need financial assistance —and it is our job as an organization to assist them. But we (farmers) must also try to pull ourselves up by our bootstraps too!

Sign-ups for the federal drought relief package began on October 3. While most farmers hoped their yields would be high enough that they would not have to apply, they were grateful that the aid was there if needed. The IFB kept its members abreast of details regarding relief so that anyone who was interested in applying could do so.

From the 1960s until 1991, the building at 130 E. Washington Street in Indianapolis was home to Indiana Farm Bureau and Farm Bureau Insurance.

FARM BUREAU INSURANCE

Chapter Seven
Coping With Change

In November 1988, as the drought faded, Farm Bureau Insurance Companies announced its plans to develop a new headquarters in Indianapolis. The existing five-story building, formerly home to the Indianapolis Rubber Company, was located on 8.6 acres at Georgia and East streets. Plans called for complete renovation of the building, along with the addition of two floors. Construction was to begin in mid-1989, with completion set for early 1991. The offices of Indiana Farm Bureau, Inc., would also be housed in the building, on the seventh floor.

August 1989 ground breaking ceremonies were conducted at Farm Bureau's new state headquarters site. Participating in the traditional event were: (l. to r.) Tom Ulmer, Insurance executive vice president; Harry Pearson, IFB & Farm Bureau Insurance president; Ray Irvin, Indianapolis city council member; Mayor William Hudnut; Harold Garrison, chairman, Mansur Development Corp and Cornelius Alig, Mansur president.

Demolition began October 1990 for construction of a new state Farm Bureau headquarters at 225 S. East Street in Indianapolis. There were 33 separate buildings on the site that were demolished. The building formerly housed a tire manufacturer. Renovations and remodeling took two years.

The renovation took longer than planned, and the new offices, at 225 S. East Street, were ready for occupancy by April 1992. The celebratory open house on June 6 drew hundreds of visitors, including Stephen Goldsmith, mayor of Indianapolis, and Dean Kleckner, president of the AFBF.

Just a few years after the 1988 drought, another problem involving water received a great deal of coverage in *The Hoosier Farmer*: wetlands and new federal legislation regarding them. Harry Pearson began by intending to write only one column on this subject in the March-April 1991 issue, and, to his surprise, he ended up writing a series of four over the next few months (and coverage of the issue continued long after that).

Traditionally, wetlands had been defined as swamps, marshes, bogs, ponds, and areas along a coast that were often covered with water. However, recent federal legislation aimed at preventing the loss of these valuable ecosystems

Many VIPs were invited to the new headquarters open house in 1992. Talking were George Doup, former IFB president; Virgil Cline, former IFB vice president; Indiana's Lt. Governor Frank O'Bannon, and former Indianapolis Mayor Bill Hudnut.

Indiana Farm Bureau and Farm Bureau Insurance began its move to new headquarters in April 1992. The extra space allowed consolidation of all company activities at one site. Twenty-two different sites were looked at before selecting the downtown site. The centralized location was termed "good for employees, members and policy holders."

went too far in the eyes of many, not only in defining "wetlands" but in punishing those who disturbed the so-called wetlands on their private property.

Pearson called these new regulations "one of the greatest challenges to private property rights since homesteading made possible the settling of America by our ancestors decades ago." He declared that very few people were opposed to the protection of true wetlands, "but serious questions are raised when wooded lands and forests located on dark soils where water never stands or land that has been farmed in the past is now being called wetlands."

In his columns, he recounted many horror stories of private citizens, many of them farmers, who, unaware of new strict regulations, had tried to improve their property but ended up in jail and with heavy fines levied against them.

"Fines for violating arbitrarily created wetlands regulations are more severe than those given for fraud, burglary, larceny, auto theft and drug offenses," he wrote in the March-April 1991 issue. "The real issue is not wetlands but the taking of private property without compensation."

Farm Bureau had long had a policy on preserving true wetlands—as long as private property was protected and economic development was enhanced. The new regulations did not do that, however. Furthermore, they arbitrarily declared many areas to be wetlands in a way that seemed to have no sense to it. Pearson declared that these regulations were a threat to all landowners, not just farmers:

> ...anyone who owns property if it includes areas that have arbitrarily been determined to include wetlands. The implications are far reaching and the paperwork, fees, permits and potential delays of improving one's own property promises to forever deny the dreams of many small landowners. (*The Hoosier Farmer*, May-June 1991)

Thanks to the hue and cry raised by the IFB and other Farm Bureaus around the country, the federal government took another look at the original wetlands regulations, which had been written in 1990. The American Farm Bureau Federation reviewed the delineation manual, the guide to wetlands regulations, and offered some suggestions for its revision. Jim Barnett, IFB natural resources director, participated in this effort. The IFB received almost 5,000 letters and phone calls of support from its members regarding revision of the manual.

But revision of the manual did not halt the controversy. Pearson told the 1991 IFB convention that

> It should come as no surprise to anyone, then, that some of the bureaucrats, and the "extreme" environmentalists (most environ-

Phoenix hosted the 1990 American Farm Bureau convention. U.S. Vice President and Indiana native Dan Quayle, left, spoke to more than 3,000 farmers and guests. Accompanying Quayle to the stage were Harry Pearson, IFB president, and U.S. Senator Richard Lugar.

mentalists are great to work with) have already charged that the revised delineation manual is strictly a political document, with no scientific basis. Neither should it be a surprise then—that the acreage figures used by them—to cite wetland losses are outdated—and grossly exaggerated. The idea that the 1989 manual is purely "scientific" and was done without political influence—is just as ludicrous. The truth is, that "wetlands policy" is already way ahead of "wetlands science" and the bureaucrats have already taken control of the issue from the scientists. (*The Hoosier Farmer*, January-February 1992)

In the summer of 1992, the Supreme Court ruled that government action that diminishes the value of private property is, as the Farm Bureau had said in connection with wetlands regulation, a "taking" within the meaning of the Fifth Amendment. Therefore, the IFB helped to draft and successfully lobby for legislation that would require Indiana's attorney general to evaluate all administrative rules proposed by a state agency to determine if it would adversely affect the private property rights of Indiana residents. The federal debate regarding wetlands continued, however.

With the advent of the 1990s, change seemed to accelerate throughout American society. The IFB was no exception, as it and its related companies underwent many changes at the start of the decade.

A major streamlining took place within the Farm Bureau Insurance Companies after the companies experienced some major difficulties with the underwriting structure of the casualty company in the late 1980s. As Harry Pearson told the 1990 IFB convention, the changes within the organization would improve efficiency and customer service:

> In matching the talents of people with new responsibilities and offering more training, our companies will be more efficient, provide faster service and deliver a diversity of products based on customer needs. It's imperative that we look at the work that we do from the perspective of the customer and the member. (*The Hoosier Farmer*, January-February 1991)

Don Henderson, then vice president of the IFB, was appointed to serve as interim CEO during the transition period. Clyde Turbeville was later hired as CEO of the insurance companies.

Within 16 months of Turbeville's becoming CEO, the casualty company had reversed its downward course and its financial health had rebounded. Even with paying $3 million as part of the reinsurance costs for Hurricane Andrew, the company was in better shape than it had been for years. (In 1996, however, the insurance companies suffered a one-day loss of $19 million, which led to one of its worst years on record. However, 1997 promised to be better, thanks to a dedicated staff and, they hoped, no large storm losses.)

The life insurance company, which had not been affected by the casualty company problems, was also in very good shape in 1993. Ward Financial Group recognized it as one of the top 50 outstanding insurers in the country, based on its performance, financial security, and consistency of results from 1987 through 1991.

In 1993, the IFB and the Farm Bureau Insurance Companies offered a special retirement package to their employees. A dozen individuals took advantage of the offer, taking with them 291 years of service and experience in various aspects of IFB operation. Their length of service ranged from 33 to 14 years.

During the IFB's 75th annual convention, President Harry Pearson cited them, saying,

> Seldom in the history of state Farm Bureaus, in Indiana or across the nation, can we spotlight so many employees who have made such a contribution. They serve as an example of all the good that individuals can accomplish working selflessly for the benefit of others...It was a fitting tribute that they be honored during the 75th anniversary because many of our program achievements are directly related to their efforts during their years of employment. They leave a tremendous legacy of accomplishments. (*The Hoosier Farmer*, January-February 1994)

Producers Marketing Association underwent a drastic change when it joined with Michigan Livestock Exchange. During this time of deregulation, expansion within the livestock industry, and consolidation within the meat packing industry, joining forces with another cooperative made good economic sense and would make it possible to deal more effectively and efficiently with rapid change. As Pearson told the 1990 annual convention of the IFB:

> Packer concentration, vertical integration, direct marketing, price discovery, are all issues that are increasingly difficult to deal with in today's market environment, and they were looked at. Joining forces with another livestock agency makes it possible to deal more effectively with these issues. The combining of numbers (volume) in the marketplace is beneficial to the producer. (*The Hoosier Farmer*, January-February 1991)

The IFB had taken over the management of PMA in 1970 after it faced financial ruin. In 1987, the IFB purchased PMA and transformed it into a corporation, which meant it was no longer a tax-exempt cooperative association. By restructuring as a corporation owned by IFB, the inquiries for preferred stock redemption could be honored. With the stock valued at 23¢ on the dollar, many dollars were returned to original investors or their heirs.

The sale of Indiana's Producers Marketing Association was consummated January 3, 1994. PMA, one of Indiana's major livestock marketing agencies, returned to a patron cooperative after being purchased by Michigan Livestock Exchange. Consolidations in the meatpacking industry, coupled with fewer producers were a driving force in the transaction. Signing sale documents were IFB president Harry Pearson, left, and Tom Reed, MLE president.

The new logo appeared at sites soon after PMA's sale to Michigan Livestock Exchange. Advertisements stated: "A new name, new look and a proven concept should bring Indiana livestock producers higher profits." Indiana Livestock Exchange's backbone was the sales coordinators at MLE headquarters who negotiated with regional packers to obtain the highest possible price for producers.

By 1990, to gain efficiencies of operation for PMA, the IFB searched for another regional cooperative to manage PMA.

Michigan Livestock Exchange was interested in this task from the start, seeing joint operations with PMA as a way to help both organizations extend their reach and prosper. The MLE also believed they had an ethical obligation to assist another cooperative weather hard times. IFB contracted with MLE to manage the PMA facilities in July 1990.

From the outset, the agreement was beneficial to both organizations. It gave PMA access to credit and capital through the Livestock Feeding Program, the Michigan Livestock Credit Corporation (MLCC), and Payment Plus (SM). MLCC received a $1 million loan from the Farm Bureau Life Insurance Co. According to *Pride in the Past, Faith in the Future*, a history of the Michigan Livestock Exchange,

> Over the next three years PMA grew rapidly in both volume and market outlets. Livestock volume grew from about a half-million head in 1990 to nearly 1.4 million, including 1.2 million hogs, in 1993. In 1992, PMA doubled in size with the purchase of a group of successful hog marketing stations owned by Jack and Joe Judge and known as Hoosier Stockyards. The same year, PMA posted a $280,000 profit, its first since 1972. By the end of 1993 MLE had achieved its goal and was ready to restore PMA to cooperative status. (pg. 179)

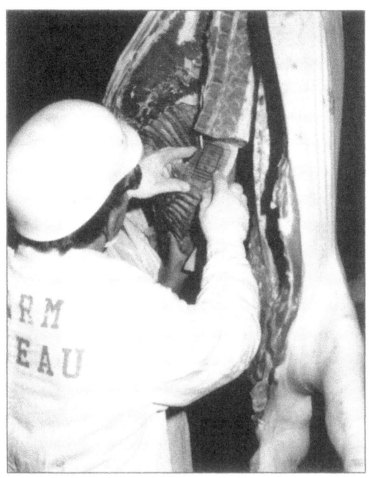

Indiana Farm Bureau's Commodity Department staff helped evaluate more than 7,000 hogs in 1990 measuring length, loin eye, percent fat, color and marbling. The top hog would be named Hog of the Year with the producer cited at the state convention.

Then, on January 3, 1994, MLE bought PMA from the IFB and renamed it Indiana Livestock Exchange. With the purchase, MLE took ownership of the 24 PMA markets in Indiana. Harry Pearson, president of IFB, also became a board member of MLE.

The merger was successful. By mid-year, ILE's livestock feeding program had placed $62 million worth of livestock on Indiana and Michigan farms. Under this program, ILE placed livestock on the farms to be raised by the farmers. When the cattle or hogs were later marketed, the ILE deducted the initial cost. In this way, farmers could continue raising livestock without a huge initial investment.

In addition, by 1995, ILE marketed more than $700 million worth of livestock and entered into an agreement with Thorn Apple Valley, a Detroit meat

packing operation, to supply all their hogs for the next decade—4.4 million animals a year. Such an agreement would not have been possible had MLE and PMA not joined forces.

Unfortunately, Thorn Apple curtailed it slaughter operations in 1998, which ended the agreement. During that same year, MLE had also merged into the Southern States Cooperative, headquartered in Richmond, Virginia, and the MLE board then became an advisory board to the SSC.

The Indiana Farm Bureau Cooperative Association was also not immune from drastic change during this time. As with the other IFB-related organizations, it was decided to find a way to improve efficiency and marketing. To that end, in late 1991 the IFBCA merged with Countrymark, a cooperative that covered Ohio and Michigan. With this merger, the IFB president no longer had a seat on the cooperatives board and the IFBCA no longer existed by the name it had proudly carried for more than 50 years. However, it continued to provide the same cooperative services and products it had before the merger.

Countrymark also later underwent some massive changes. A $43 million employee buyout in 1996 harmed the company's finances, and that was followed the next year by a multimillion-dollar loss in its turkey business. In order to survive, Countrymark was merged with Land O' Lakes, a super-regional farm co-op, in 1998. Land O' Lakes took over management of Countrymark's $1 billion seed, feed, and fertilizer businesses and its grain handling. However, it did not take over Countrymark's Mount Vernon oil refinery and fuel sales.

In the early and mid-1990s, the IFB itself continued its tradition of keeping farmers informed and up-to-date on any situation that could affect them. One new service was a weekly newsletter designed to quickly report essential commodity news so that farmers could make informed marketing decisions. It included prices, trends, and outlooks on corn, soybeans, wheat, hogs,

Indiana Farm Bureau has been a long time supporter of the Indiana State Fair and 4-H livestock sale. Participating in the 4-H Sale of Champions on behalf of Farm Bureau Insurance in 1990 was Jack Heaton, public relations; Harry Pearson, IFB president; and Burt Taylor, operations senior vice president.

Former Indiana Governor Otis Bowen, M.D., visited with Harry Pearson, IFB president, during the 1992 IFB convention.

In 1992 U.S. Senator Dan Coates dropped by during an IFB board of directors meeting. From left are: Larry Boys, Don Henderson, Mike Zimmerman, Herb Likens, Coates, Paul Ketner, Harry Pearson, Carol Hegel, Jerry Arburn, Arvel Borcherding, Rita Sharma, Lowell Badger, Wayne Bode and Merlin Funk.

U. S. President George Bush, right, discussed some relevant farm issues with Harry Pearson, IFB president. The 1992 visit took place during the AFBF national convention.

At the 1994 American Farm Bureau national convention in St. Louis, Missouri, Harry Pearson, IFB president, greeted U.S. Senator Bob Dole (R-Kansas). Dole was guest speaker at the general session.

*The North American Free Trade Agreement (better known as NAFTA)
was passed by Congress in November 1993. A formidable grass roots
effort generated the support necessary for congressional passage. Going
the "extra mile" was former Delaware County president Joe Russell who
"carved" his view on NAFTA into one of his harvested soybean fields.*

and cattle. The first issue went out to subscribers in March 1994. The newsletter, which was coordinated by the Agricultural Development & Natural Resources Division, was aimed at those farms that had not signed up for the computerized Data Transmission Network market services, which provided a more comprehensive look at markets via personal computers in farm homes.

The rapid pace of regulatory change continued into the mid-1990s, leaving farmers often confused about their legal rights and responsibilities in regard to environmental law. *The Hoosier Farmer* frequently reported accounts of farmers and other landowners around the country who found themselves in legal trouble, often innocently, over such issues. Therefore, in November 1994, the IFB published *Environmental Laws and Regulations—Indiana Agricultural Handbook*. It was co-edited by Jim Barnett, IFB director of Natural Resources, and Joe Miller, IFB environmental legal counsel. Miller said the handbook was setting a

One of the first IFB Environmental LAWS & Regulations Handbooks was presented to U.S. Senator Richard Lugar during the 1994 state convention. Lugar lauded its importance to Indiana farmers during a media conference. The book was complied and updated by IFB staff.

precedent; he knew of no other publication that discussed agriculture laws for farmers. The chapters covered many topics, including storage tanks, pesticide disposal, spill reporting, wetlands regulations, worker protection standards, and confined feeding.

The handbook was designed as a reference manual that would be updated quarterly, with additions covering changes in laws and regulations. According to *The Hoosier Farmer*, the handbook "has been met with enthusiasm, gratitude, and in many cases, daily use."

Media interviews are a common occurrence for the president of Farm Bureau. In 1994 Jeff Swaitek, Indianapolis Star/News interviewed Harry Pearson at the state headquarters and spent some time on the Pearson farm in Blackford County. The feature story appeared in a Sunday edition.

Membership growth has always been one measure of success within Farm Bureau. A key factor to increasing numbers is the Insurance Company. Helping celebrate another successful year in 1994 with a "100% membership celebration" cake were Harry Pearson, IFB president, and Clyde Turbeville, Insurance executive vice president and CEO.

During the 1995 IFB convention's Sunday evening Vespers, Carol Hegel, IFB second vice president; U.S. Senator Richard Lugar; and Jerry Arburn, IFB vice president, discuss current agricultural events.

George Doup, retired IFB president, and U.S. Congressman David McIntosh were among the 2,000 members and guests at the 1995 IFB convention's banquet.

The IFB, through the Women's Division, also published another informative book at this time, targeted to another audience. This was a coloring book that told the story of how a variety of farm products came to be part of a pizza. Sadly, many children in the mid-1990s had no clear idea that their food did not magically spring up in grocery stores but had to be grown and raised on farms. Pizza was chosen because it is one of America's favorite foods and because many of the products found in a typical pizza are grown in Indiana: wheat for the crust, tomatoes for the sauce, milk for cheese, cattle and hogs for meat, as well as vegetables like peppers and onions.

An annual teachers workshop conducted by the IFB state women's committee started in 1996. Forty elementary teachers learned about IFB's school programs and hands-on classroom projects.

The Women's Division, along with the Information and Public Relations Division, began in the 1990s to also produce videos to educate schoolchildren about beef, dairy, hogs, corn, and wheat production. The 1999 Emmy award winning video was "Exploring Planet Pizza."

A new educational project with IFB involvement began in 1994, when the Center for Agricultural Science & Heritage was incorporated as a not-for-profit organization. Also known as The Barn, the 23-acre center is located directly across from the Indiana State Fairgrounds in Indianapolis. When completed, it will bring together the rural heritage of the nation with the science and technology of farming that are shaping the future.

Demand for "Farming the Classroom" barns exceeded expectations. Originally intended for a one-time March Agriculture Day blitz by IFB's women's committee in 92 counties, it became so popular an additional 280 had to be ordered. Barns contained videos, pamphlets, brochures, and other teaching aids. By 1991, County Farm bureau volunteers had reached some 500,000 school age children from kindergarten through 4th grade. Carol Hegel, left, IFB women's committee chair, and Eleanor Uhde, classroom volunteer, display an assembled barn.

The cornerstone of the center will be the Normandy Barn, which was built in 1936 to house prize-winning Guernseys and was later operated by Purdue University for a time. Although slated for demolition, the barn was saved, relocated to the new site, and renovated with funding provided by the General Assembly. The Normandy Barn will serve as the program development base of the center and as a multi-purpose facility for events, classes, and other activities.

The center will also include a 55,000-square-foot visitors facility, which will offer creative and entertaining exhibits to engage visitors in learning about agriculture and the food supply. The staff will develop curriculum-based activities, tours, guides, and publications. Outreach programming will interact with students, teachers, and agriculture groups.

IFB president Harry Pearson, right, presented Indiana Governor Evan Bayh a "symbolic" membership card during the 1995 state convention's delegate session.

Also to be located at the center will be a farmer's market, a greenhouse, outdoor demonstration and exhibit area, and agricultural business complex.

The total cost of the center, including an initial operating endowment, will be $20 million. In 1998, the center was seeking to raise $10 million in private donations, with an equal match from government sources. Tom Asher, director of the IFB Information/Public Relations Division, is a member of The Barn's board of trustees. They held their first meeting in February 1999.

Task forces have long been used by many organizations to study complex subjects and report to the membership-at-large on their findings. Given the rapidly growing complexity of many issues related to agriculture in the 1990s, the IFB formed several of its own task forces. Composed of IFB members from throughout the state, the task forces met regularly to study these issues and inform the rest of the membership.

In 1995, there were four task forces in operation: government services delivery, planning and zoning, drainage, and property taxes (yes, even after almost 30 years of fighting for property tax reform, the IFB was still working on it; several reforms had been instituted over the years, but none was sufficient or fair, the IFB believed.)

Another task force investigated land-use issues, which had become a crucial issue in recent years, beginning with the wetlands regulations and expanding from there to encompass property rights as a whole. Harry Pearson defined this struggle to the 1995 IFB convention:

> There is a debate underway in this country today, and it's been going on for some time, that would undermine this very basic and fundamental right. That discussion centers around ways to slowly "define away" private property rights.
>
> Notice I didn't say "take away"; I said "define away," because you, as a property owner, still have your name on the deed, make bank payments, and pay the property taxes. But by "redefining," someone else now tells you what you can or cannot do with that property.
>
> Call a fence line an overgrowth of trees and brush, and it belongs to you; but call it a habitat for rabbits and birds, and it belongs to everyone. Call the wet area on a farm a swamp or a mudhole and it's yours, yet designate it a wetland and it belongs to everyone. (*The Hoosier Farmer*, January-February 1996)

Property issues had expanded to include the ownership of abandoned railroad rights-of-way. While railroads had once been the major form of long-distance transportation in the country, they had in large part been replaced, or railroad companies had consolidated, leaving abandoned tracks crisscrossing many areas of the country, including large expanses of farmland. In the 1980s, ownership of these rights-of-way came into question as many groups sought to own them. Many of them were purchased to be turned into recreational trails, in the "rails to trails" move-

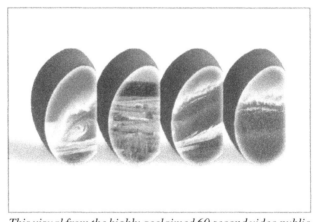

This visual from the highly acclaimed 60 second video public service spot ended with a tiny sliver (1/32nd) of the peeling. A voice says: "If we peel this last section, it represents the amount of soil on the earth's surface that we depend on to grow crops to feed the entire world." Used extensively by Indiana TV stations, the audio was rewritten for radio.

IFB's District 8 woman leader Linda Bacon, Rush County, accepted her county's award from AFBF president Dean Kleckner for the Rush County Farm Bureau's Idea Exchange T-shirt project in 1996. Ceremonies took place during the AFBF convention.

Indiana Farm Bureau and Ivy Tech State College teamed together to rename Ivy Tech's Indianapolis headquarters in memory of former IFB vice president/ secretary and Ivy Tech president Glenn Sample. A statewide campaign launched in 1996 raised $100,000 to fund a memorial endowment to underwrite a new faculty development program. Spearheading the campaign were Harry Pearson, IFB president, and Gerald Lamkin, Ivy Tech president.

Frank O'Bannon was elected Indiana's governor November 1996. IFB president Harry Pearson briefed the governor on some key ag issues and acquainted him with Farm Bureau policy positions. Issues included the property tax burden on farmers and protecting farmland.

Farm Bureau supports many facets of education. It cosponsors the Indiana Teacher of the Year along with the Indiana Department of Education, IFB Insurance Companies and Scholastic, Inc. Accepting her $1,000 check at the 1996 IFB convention was 1997 Teacher of the Year Judy Fraps, right, Washington Township school system in Marion County. Looking on is Harry Pearson, IFB president, and Suellen Reed, Indiana superintendent of public instruction.

IFBee was a popular attraction during the 1996 Farmers Day Parade. After the pet parade, Indiana's Lt. Governor Frank O'Bannon congratulated the Farm Bureau mascot on a "job well done."

ment. Many farmers were concerned about this transformation. If railroad rights-of-way were to become corridors through their property, they wanted certain issues addressed, including drainage, weed control, fences, pets and livestock, farm crossings, environmental impact studies, restrooms, and drinking water.

Therefore, in 1989, delegates to the IFB convention drafted and passed a precedent-setting resolution that asked that abandoned railroad rights-of-way be returned to the adjacent property owners. (In many cases, it was not clear that the railroads had ever owned the property, which brought into question whether they could sell what they did not own.) The year after the convention delegates passed their resolution, the Indiana General Assembly passed into law HB 1071, which established transportation corridor planning boards throughout the state. County commissioners were required to approve rails-to-trails projects and other uses for the rights-of-ways before they could go forward. The law also absolved adjoining landowners of any civil liabilities from those who used the trails.

Indiana Farm Bureau's board of directors in 1996 was (l to r.) Seated: Carol Hegel, Harry Pearson, and Jerry Arburn. Back row: Wayne Bode, Mike Yoder, Merlin Funk, Larry Boys, Rita Sharma, Herb Likens, Lowell Badger, Paul Ketner, Randy Kron, and Arvel Borcherding.

In the 1990s, IFB members in many counties around the state, who were used to the process of gathering together for policy development, used this law to prevent unwise uses of various abandoned rights-of-way. The IFB it-self became deeply involved in several class action suits to determine the respective rights of underlying property owners and railroad interests when the railroads abandon their tracks and rights-of-way. The AFBF soon joined the IFB in this struggle and helped to gain national attention for the issue.

Jerry Chandler, left, Hendricks County, was interviewed by ABC's Good Morning America crew. The video taping with Shiela Kast dealt with Farm Bureau's position on the "rails to trails" issue.

American Farm Bureau vice president Carl Loop, left, presents IFB vice president Jerry Arburn with the AFBF Gold Star Award during the 1996 national convention. Honors were cited for 13 different categories.

At IFB's annual county presidents meeting in Indianapolis, Indiana Lt. Governor Joe Kernan was greeted by Harry Pearson, IFB president. Newly elected Kernan also served as commissioner of agriculture. He was formerly mayor of South Bend.

Harry Pearson, white hat, IFB president, donned boots, chaps and spurs to participate with 250 other riders in the kick-off trail ride/parade for the 1996 Hoosier Horse Fair. Accompanying President Pearson is Tom Asher, IFB Information & Public Relations Division. The trip started in downtown Indianapolis and ended at the state fairgrounds on 38th Street.

"Kill the Death Tax" was the slogan for a national Farm Bureau program. Farmers were encouraged to contact their U.S. representatives in Washington, D.C., urging repeal of the death tax. Under the current law, many farm families had to sell all or part of their farms to pay the punitive federal estate taxes. Indiana farmers wrote 7,500 letters. Nationally the AFBF campaign generated some 70,000 letters urging reforms.

Tax issues-estate and capital gains taxes were the top priority to the 1997 Washington, D.C. trip. Fountain County FB members were from U.S. congressional district 7. (l. to r.) Fountain County president Sam Allen; District 3 Young Farmer representative Sherry Underwood; FB district 5 woman leader Joan Truax; IFB staffer Mari Howard; District 5 young farmer Donnie Lamb; Vigo County president Terry Hayhurst; Rep Ed Pease, R-Indiana; and District 3 young farmer representative Kevin Underwood.

Indiana Farm Bureau had an exhibit at the 1997 World Pork Expo. The display focused on several activities but highlighted IFB's "kill the death tax." Attendees were encouraged to write letters to the U.S. congressional representatives requesting repeal of the federal inheritance tax. Bob Cherry, IFB government relations, and Paul Hoffman, regional field representative, explain the project to a prospective letter writer.

Another issue that began receiving a great deal of concerned attention at this time was the rapid loss of farmland. Between 1982 and 1992, Indiana lost more than 150,000 acres of farm land to other uses, a rate of about 40 acres a day. A 1994 study indicated that Indiana had lost 5 percent of its farm land to industrial and housing development during the previous two years. A national study presented the grim statistic that 1.57 million acres of farm land were being gobbled up across the country every year—that's three acres every minute. Although the amount of land devoted to farming had been shrinking since the Farm Bureau was created in 1919, the rapid pace of the loss in recent years was startling and worrisome. (The one bright spot was that one farmer could now feed 129 people, whereas in 1930, even though more farm land was available, he could feed only 24.)

In 1995, Harry Pearson appointed a Farmland Preservation Task Force to study the loss and preservation of Hoosier farmland. The main challenge in this issue was to balance the rights of property owners to manage their property as they chose, including selling it, with the preservation of farm land. After a period of study, the 16-member task force made two basic recommendations: to begin an educational campaign to tell the public about the importance of preserving farmland and to create a state-level task force that would bring together government officials, real estate developers, planners, environmental groups, and others with farmers to find workable solutions.

However, even farmers were not united on how farmland should be used, which complicated the situation:

> As economic development occurs, urban growth consumes productive farmland. Economic development broadens the tax base and increases the demand for property. That increases the cost of land. High costs can make things tough on heirs because of the increased burden of inheritance and estate taxes. High cost is also a barrier to new farmers because land is a necessary input cost for agriculture.
>
> The issue results in competing interests among the agricultural community—and a dilemma for Farm Bureau. Some farmers want to see economic development controlled but not discouraged. Their primary concern is the right to dispose of, develop and freely use property, and weighs against other concerns to protect and preserve farmland. (*The Hoosier Farmer*, March-April 1997)

Despite all the differences, there was, in the end, only one consideration for the use of farm land. David C. Ford, IFB general counsel, summed up that consideration in *The Hoosier Farmer*, "Things that grow on the land are renewable, but the land itself is not. We can't grow more land. We'll have to think about being careful with what we have."

American Farm Bureau President Dean Kleckner, right, discussed federal legislation with IFB President Harry Pearson, left, and Purdue University dean of agriculture Vic Lechtenberg during a 1997 visit in W. Lafayette. Sessions on the agenda ranged from staff presentations on distance education, academic programs, land use, animal waste handling, precision farming, food safety, federal research money and Food System 21.

Members of the 1997 IFB board of directors were: (l. to r.) Front row: Wayne Bode, Mike Yoder, Harry Pearson, Jerry Arburn, Carol Hegel, and George Corya. Back row: Merlin Funk, Larry Boys, Rita Sharma, Herb Likens, Don Villwock, Gary Reding, and Randy Kron.

The task force apparently succeeded in their educational efforts. In the 1998 session, the General Assembly passed Senate Bill 445, "Nonconforming Uses of Agricultural Land." While the IFB did not create the bill, it was instrumental in getting it passed. Kendall Culp, president of the Jasper County Farm Bureau, suggested a model for the bill to State Sen. Katie Wolf, who took the concept to the General Assembly.

IFBee, Indiana Farm Bureau's mascot, took membership recruitment to a new level at the 1997 AFBF national convention.

The existence of this law meant that a county or municipality may not use its planning or zoning process to interfere with existing agricultural operations. It does not infringe upon a community's right to adopt a comprehensive plan or zoning ordinance, but it created a uniform, statewide variance to them. This bill would protect farmers faced with development creeping in around them, where the new neighbors were offended by agricultural operations, such as farm machinery on the roads or the normal odor of livestock production.

By the 1990s, the IFB and many farmers had long ago incorporated computers into their operations. As the use of computers and the scope of what they could do increased, the Farm Bureau likewise enhanced its use of computers and computerized information.

One such use was the specialized business support and accounting information handled by the IFB Service Company. A specialized, farmer-designed program called Agmaster, which the Service Company sold and supported, provided comprehensive financial, farm tax, and credit and management information.

General Colin Powell, right, USA (ret.) chairman of the Joint Chiefs of Staff from 1989 to 1993, was keynote speaker at the 1997 AFBF convention in Nashville, Tennessee. During a reception Harry Pearson, IFB president, visited with the general. Powell spoke about his 35 years in the U.S. Army and talked about the benefits of a freer world trade.

Farm Bureau hosted the U.S. senatorial candidates on Farmers Day (August 19, 1998) at the Indiana State Fair prior to the Farmers Day Parade. The event took place in the Farm Bureau Building. Candidates appeared separately. In the above photo is Harry Pearson, IFB president; and Paul Helmke, third term mayor of Ft. Wayne. In the photo below is Pearson with eventual winner, Evan Bayh, two-term Indiana governor. Bayh was the nation's youngest governor at age 33 when elected in 1989. Discussion topics included Food Quality Protection Act, international trade, fast track negotiating and capital gains tax repeal.

The Internet also came to play an important role in the communications of Farm Bureaus around the country. The AFBF created a Website at www.fb. com in early 1996. Called "The Voice of Agriculture" and updated daily, this site provides the latest AFBF news and commentary and provides links with state and county Farm Bureaus, agricultural educational material, and other ag-related resources, such as the National 4-H Council and the National FFA.

Purdue and Ohio State Universities joined forces that same year to create Ag Answers, which provides answers and advice on agriculture-related problems. It is available via email or at the Purdue Website www.aes. purdue.edu.

In addition, the Internet itself quickly became a way for farmers to learn about things like weather conditions, markets, planting and harvesting issues. It also offers a way for farmers from around the globe to communicate and connect with one another.

The IFB created its own homepage on the World Wide Web at www.farmbureau.com. In addition to offering a way for the IFB and its members to communicate with each other, it was also designed to teach the general public about agriculture and the Farm Bureau.

St. Joseph County FB members participated in Enviroquest 1997. Guests were area 6th graders from area schools. Programs were on environment and what can be done to preserve it. Farm Bureau displayed the "softer footsteps" exhibit and described farming methods to protect the earth and keep foods safe.

Jim & Jane Gillooly, left, Washington, received the AgriAmerica Network's Farmer of the Year award from network director Gary Truitt during the 1997 IFB state convention. "We chose Mr. Gillooly not for which side of the issue he is on, but rather for his courage and willingness to become involved," Truitt said. "It is producers like this who will get informed and get involved that we will need to meet the challenges of the next century."

The 1998 IFB Resolutions Committee considered county policy submissions. At times, county recommendations have strong and divided opinions on some issues that the committee has to resolve. The committee also exercises the discipline necessary to keep policy relevant to Farm Bureau's purpose. Members are: (l. to r.) Front row: Donnie Lamb, Boone; Lurinda Smith, Rush; Tom Pugh, Parke; Richard Fritz, Allen; Kenneth Krebbs, Brown; Eleanor Laffoon-Altepeter; D3 woman leader; and Paul Ooley, Lawrence. Second row: Pam Kobelt, Floyd; Herb Likens, D6 director; Jim Cherry, Hancock; Tom Smith, Fulton; Doug Horn, Jay; Mike Beard, Clinton; and Kay Kemper, Tipton. Third row: Jerry Arburn, IFB vice president and committee chair; Tony Schroeder, Gibson; Keven Lorenz, Clark; Mark Seib, Posey; Steve Smith, Madison; Randy Kron, D9 director; and Donnie Lawson, Boone.

A 1998 ceremonial signing took place in the governor's office creating a public governing body for the Center for Agricultural Science and Heritage better known as The BARN. Seated from left are Senator Katie Wolfe, Senator Tom Weatherwax, Governor Frank O'Bannon, Representative Bill Friend and Senator Jim Lewis. Back row from left are: BARN director of operations Betsy Kranz; Steve Panke, BARN board member; Wayne Dillman, BARN board; member; Dick Thompson, consultant; Harry Pearson, IFB; John Baugh, Purdue; Cress Hizer, Indiana Grain & Feed Association president; and Joe Pearson. deputy commissioner of agriculture.

Indiana farmers from almost every county contributed hay to fellow farmers/ranchers in hay-short states. Many times the hay was credited with survival of the farmers livestock operations. Hay was shipped to Texas, Carolinas, and Oklahoma.

Lynn Johnson, AFBF young farmer chairman, congratulated Lebanon's Don and Jodie Lamb. The Lambs were cited for being in the Young Farmer Achievement Award top five. The Lambs won free use of a Case IH tractor for 250 hours. Activities took place at the 1998 AFBF convention.

The 1998 Oklahoma project, dubbed "Hoosier Hay Lift," involved 1,200 farmers from 40 of Indiana's 92 counties. Some 20,000 square and round bales were trucked or barged to needy ranchers.

Dean Kleckner, AFBF president, was a panelist at Purdue's Farm Forecast that dealt with agriculture's future. Other panelists' organizations included Farmland Industries, Dow AgroSciences, Pioneer and Dupont. Kleckner talked with Meredith Kincaid, Hendricks County FB president; and Don Paarlburg, Purdue professor emeritus of agriculture economics.

IFB's "Farming the Classroom" volunteers use "edutainment" to help elementary students understand the importance of farmers and agriculture in their everyday life. By 1991, more than a half million Hoosier students had been told ag's story by trained volunteers. Teaching is Janet Kemper of Tippecanoe County.

The Web site, created in 1997, contains areas for kids; an educational area aimed at teachers, which explains the school speakers program called "Farming the Classroom"; a government and legislation section; an agricultural markets section; a calendar of events; and a media section that displays recent IFB news releases. One area of the News section is aimed directly at non-farmers, to inform them of people, issues, and events related to farming.

Even though it was now taking advantage of the latest technology to stay in touch with members, the IFB never forgot the best, and oldest, form of communication: face-to-face gatherings where everyone has a say. In 1997, the organization's grassroots traditions were strengthened with a pilot program called Local Issue Focus Teams, or LIFT, coordinated by the Government Relations Division. With an eventual goal of 100 teams, the first ones were formed in Bartholomew, Boone, Daviess, Decatur, Elkhart, Grant, Jackson, Jennings, Madison, Posey, Pulaski, Randolph, Tippecanoe, Vigo, and Whitley counties in order to meet regularly and search for action-oriented solutions to various problems.

The teams met in each other's home to form study circles, which were open to adults of any age. Armed with current information on a variety of issues, both immediate and long-term, they would discuss the issues as well as possible solutions. Afterward, they would send their comments to IFB to be read and incorporated into member service, education, and public affairs programs, as well as policy development. Since team members came from all areas of their counties, they were considered a reliable indication of the sentiments there.

While all IFB members had the opportunity to have their voices heard, the voices of LIFT members were "amplified," since their suggestions were to be given particular attention. Input from LIFT was not meant to replace policy development in the counties, long a mainstay of IFB organization, but to serve as suggestions to be considered.

Doles and Pearsons visited briefly during the 1998 American Farm Bureau national convention in Charlotte, North Carolina. Elizabeth Dole, left, delivered the keynote address at the morning session. She was president of the American Red Cross. Accompanying her is her husband who was former U.S. Senator and Republican presidential candidate Robert Dole. In the center were Harry, IFB president, and Betty Jo Pearson.

In addition to suggesting solutions, LIFT members could also take part in committees that worked to carry out IFB policy and to carry out actions that would serve their community. They could also participate in other groups that worked to the benefit of all rural residents. By joining with state and county officials and programs, such groups had worked for better law enforcement, road improvement, school funding, and property tax and regulatory relief. In the late 1990s, Harry Pearson was appointed a member of Gov. O'Bannon's Citizen Commission on Taxes, which made recommendations for consideration by the General Assembly. IFB's position called for the school general fund, welfare, and inventory taxes to be removed from property taxes.

In 1999, the Indiana Farm Bureau had been in existence for 80 years. In those eight decades, the IFB had truly moved from a regional organization to one with a global reach. However, it had never lost sight of its grassroots origins, which were crucial to its continuing success. In fact, it cherished the grassroots—the members who, with their loyalty and perseverance, had kept the organization strong.

The changes that occurred during those eight decades had thoroughly transformed the world in which IFB charter members lived. From plows pulled by draft animals to self-propelled combines with computerized controls, from farms darkened by the lack of electricity to being able to "see" an entire farm from space via the Global Positioning System, from half the population being farmers to less than 2 percent—these changes and many more had changed the face of farming forever.

And so had the IFB changed, but only in ways that allowed it to maintain its vital links with its members: updated technology, more sophisticated

Members of the 1998 IFB board of directors were: (l. to r.) Seated: Bob Herrold, Jerry Arburn, Harry Pearson, Carol Hegel, and Merlin Funk. Standing: Rita Sharma, Don Villwock, Mike Yoder, Randy Kron, Gary Reding, George Corya, Herb Likens, and Larry Boys.

The 1998 state convention delegates elected Don Villwock, full time farmer from Edwardsport, Indiana Farm Bureau's vice president.

AFBF President Carl Loop presented IFB President Harry Pearson with the 12 gold star award at the 79th AFBF convention in Charlotte, North Carolina. Indiana earned the highest number possible for outstanding work in the judged categories.

communications tools, the addition of new services, and the improvement or relinquishment of old ones. What did not change was its purpose: "An organization of the farmers, by the farmers, to protect the interests of farmers; and by education, legislation and other honorable means, to promote the largest good for all the people."

Now, facing the 21st century, during which the pace of change is expected only to increase, the IFB is encountering still more challenges. How to remain relevant to members and the citizenry at large when so few families are involved in farming? How to serve the needs of its members when those needs are more diverse than ever? How to stay in touch with governments at all levels so that the interests of farmers are protected and taken into legislative consideration? How to work with many groups of citizens to preserve the remaining farmland and the way of life it has supported for countless generations? In a time when many children do not understand that food comes from farms, how to ensure that those who know little, if anything, about agriculture will not only respect the work that farmers do but also understand the need to protect it?

The Indiana Farm Bureau has endured for so long because of a quick adaptability that rests on a solid foundation of like-minded people gathered together for the common good. As long as there are farmers in the Hoosier state, there will be an Indiana Farm Bureau to serve them.

Don Villwock, center, IFB D7 director, voiced support for an AFBF policy position during the 1998 AFBF convention. Listening were Gary Reding, left, D8 director; and Randy Kron, right, D9 director.

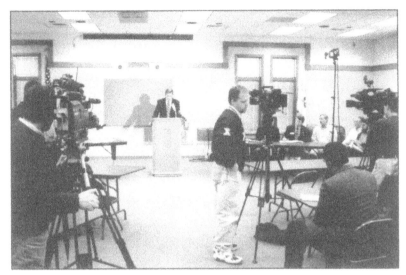

The pork crisis in late 1998 and early 1999 impacted nearly every hog producer in America. Record lows of $8 per hundred were having tragic consequences on hog producers. Many counties cooperated to get the message to consumers and officials on just how serious it was. A media conference was conducted by District 3 FB counties. Alan Kemper, Tippecanoe County FB president, offers background information to media from Lafayette and Indianapolis.

A "Taste from Indiana Farms" was a three-day tradition during the Indiana State Fair. Sponsored by IFB's state women's committee, each district was responsible for a particular food commodity. Available samples and nutritional information plus information on Indiana agriculture were provided to some 8,000 fair visitors annually. The event took place in the Farm Bureau Building's auditorium.

Manning the STOP (Stop Taxing Our Property) booth during the 1998 IFB state convention were Phil Springstun, Warrick County president; and Alan Kemper, Tippecanoe County president. Materials were available to assist members write letters to their state representatives.

Indiana Farm Bureau's Bob Kraft, government relations division, uses a visual to reinforce the IFB's position that property taxes are unfair to agriculture. The media event took place in the Farm Bureau Building during the Indiana State Fair in 1998.

Indiana Farm Bureau officially launched the STOP (Stop Taxing Our Property) campaign November 1998 with a media conference. Robert Kraft, IFB government relations, announced findings of a poll of 600 Hoosier voters, who were asked for opinions on property, income, sales and gas taxes. Also answering reporter questions were Harry Pearson, IFB president; Wayne Dillman, Indiana Farmers Union; and Meredith Kincaid, Hendricks County FB president.

Celebrities met during the 1998 Indiana State Fair Farmers Day Parade when IFBee, mascot for Indiana Farm Bureau, says "howdy" to Indiana's Lt. Governor Joe Kernan, who is also Indiana's commissioner of agriculture.

Indiana Farm Bureau "maxed" at the AFBF national convention with 12 gold stars, the top number possible in the award categories. Accepting the plaque is IFB President Harry Pearson, left, from Dean Kleckner, AFBF president.

IFB's state young farmer committee visited the Indiana State House and talked with Senator David Ford (R-Hartford City) in the visitors' gallery of the Senate chamber. One of the young farmers' primary concerns was property tax relief during the 1999 legislative session.

LaPorte County FB women conducted a food checkout day. One of many held throughout Indiana by county FB women's committees and other volunteers. In the foreground were from left: Dory Morley, Scipio township woman leader, Jennifer Jones, Al's East Supermarket cashier; and Wilma Marsh, county woman leader.

Harry Pearson, center, is surrounded by media when he delivered letters to Indiana Governor Frank O'Bannon during the 1999 legislative session. Land and homeowners demanding property tax relief wrote some 12,000 letters. Holding a box of letters is Robert Kraft, IFB government relations division. The letter campaign was part of IFB's "Stop Taxing Our Property (STOP)" campaign.

Appendix

A. Indiana Farm Bureau District Directors 1969 – May 1999

1969
1. Oris Bedenkop
2. George Neff
3. Lawrence Holloway
4. Carlin Schoeff
5. Marion Cowan
6. Virgil Cline
7. Edward Kuhn
8. George Ruschhaupt
9. Warren Wheaton
10. Linville Bryant

1970
1. Oris Bedenkop
2. George Neff
3. Lawrence Holloway
4. Carlin Schoeff
5. Marion Cowan
6. Virgil Cline
7. Elmo Ray
8. George Ruschhaupt
9. Warren Wheaton
10. Linville Bryant

1971
1. Oris Bedenkop
2. George Neff
3. Lawrence Holloway
4. Carlin Schoeff
5. Marion Cowan
6. Virgil Cline
7. Elmo Ray

8. George Ruschhaupt
9. Warren Wheaton
10. Linville Bryant

1972
1. Oris Bedenkop
2. George Neff
3. Lawrence Holloway
4. Carlin Schoeff
5. Marion Cowan
6. Virgil Cline
7. Elmo Ray
8. George Ruschhaupt
9. Warren Wheaton
10. Linville Bryant

1973
1. Oris Bedenkop
2. George Neff
3. Lawrence Holloway
4. Carlin Schoeff
5. Marion Cowan
6. Virgil Cline
7. Elmo Ray
8. George Ruschhaupt
9. Warren Wheaton
10. Linville Bryant

1974
1. Oris Bedenkop
2. George Neff
3. Lawrence Holloway

4. Carlin Schoeff
5. Marion Cowan
6. Virgil Cline
7. Elmo Ray
8. George Ruschhaupt
9. Warren Wheaton
10. Linville Bryant

1975
1. Oris Bedenkop
2. George Neff
3. Lawrence Holloway
4. Harry Pearson
5. Marion Cowan
6. Virgil Cline
7. Elmo Ray
8. George Ruschhaupt
9. Warren Wheaton
10. Linville Bryant

1976
1. Oris Bedenkop
2. George Neff
3. Lawrence Holloway
4. Harry Pearson
5. Marion Cowan
6. Lowell Collins
7. Elmo Ray
8. George Ruschhaupt
9. Robert Williams
10. Linville Bryant

1977

1. Oris Bedenkop
2. George Neff
3. Lawrence Holloway
4. Harry Pearson
5. Elvin Ashwill
6. Lowell Collins
7. Elmo Ray
8. George Ruschhaupt
9. Robert Williams
10. Linville Bryant

1978

1. Oris Bedenkop
2. Harold Myers
3. Lawrence Holloway
4. Harry Pearson
5. Elvin Ashwill
6. Lowell Collins
7. Elmo Ray
8. George Ruschhaupt
9. Robert Williams
10. Linville Bryant

1979

1. Oris Bedenkop*
2. Harold Myers
3. Lawrence Holloway
4. Harry Pearson
5. Elvin Ashwill
6. Lowell Collins
7. Conrad Begeman
8. Ralph Ponsler
9. Robert Williams
10. Randall Walker

* Died April 9, succeeded by Wayne Emigh (June 8).

1980

1. Wayne Emigh
2. Harold Myers
3. Lawrence Holloway
4. Harry Pearson
5. Elvin Ashwill
6. Lowell Collins
7. Conrad Begeman
8. Ralph Ponsler
9. Robert Williams
10. Randall Walker

1981

1. Wayne Emigh
2. Harold Myers
3. Lawrence Holloway
4. Harry Pearson
5. Elvin Ashwill
6. Lowell Collins
7. Conrad Begeman
8. Ralph Ponsler
9. Robert Williams
10. Randall Walker

1982

1. Wayne Emigh
2. Harold Myers
3. Lawrence Holloway
4. Harry Pearson*
5. Elvin Ashwill
6. Lowell Collins
7. Conrad Begeman
8. Ralph Ponsler
9. Robert Williams
10. Randall Walker

*Elected VP at December 1982 state convention.

1983

1. Wayne Emigh
2. Harold Myers
3. Harold Luck
4. Darlton Lavengood
5. Elvin Ashwill
6. Lowell Collins
7. Conrad Begeman
8. Ralph Ponsler
9. Robert Williams
10. Randall Walker

1984

1. Wayne Emigh
2. Harold Myers
3. Harold Luck
4. Darlton Lavengood
5. Elvin Ashwill
6. Merrill Ferris
7. Conrad Begeman
8. Ralph Ponsler
9. Robert Williams
10. Randall Walker

1985

1. Wayne Emigh
2. Harold Myers
3. Harold Luck
4. Darlton Lavengood
5. Elvin Ashwill
6. Merrill Ferris
7. Conrad Begeman
8. Ralph Ponsler
9. Robert Harper
10. Randall Walker

1986

1. Wayne Emigh
2. Harold Myers
3. Harold Luck
4. Darlton Lavengood
5. Howard Rippy
6. Merrill Ferris*
7. Conrad Begeman
8. Ralph Ponsler
9. Robert Harper
10. Randall Walker

*Died December 27

1987

1. Wayne Emigh
2. Mike Zimmerman
3. Harold Luck
4. Darlton Lavengood
5. Howard Rippy
6. Mary Ferris*
7. Conrad Begeman
8. Ralph Ponsler
9. Robert Harper
10. Randall Walker

*Elected to fill term of deceased husband.

1988

1. Wayne Emigh
2. Mike Zimmerman
3. Harold Luck
4. Darlton Lavengood
5. Howard Rippy
6. Mary Ferris
7. Lowell Badger
8. Paul Ketner

9. Jerry Arburn*
10. Arvel Borcherding

*Special election May 13.

1989

1. Wayne Bode
2. Mike Zimmerman
3. Harold Luck
4. Darlton Lavengood
5. Howard Rippy
6. Mary Ferris
7. Lowell Badger
8. Paul Ketner
9. Jerry Arburn
10. Arvel Borcherding

1990

1. Wayne Bode
2. Mike Zimmerman
3. Harold Luck
4. Larry Boys
5. Howard Rippy
6. Herb Likens
7. Lowell Badger
8. Paul Ketner
9. Jerry Arburn
10. Arvel Borcherding

1991

1. Wayne Bode
2. Mike Zimmerman
3. Harold Luck
4. Larry Boys
5. Howard Rippy
6. Herb Likens
7. Lowell Badger
8. Paul Ketner
9. Jerry Arburn
10. Arvel Borcherding

1992

1. Wayne Bode
2. Mike Zimmerman
3. Merlin Funk
4. Larry Boys
5. Rita Sharma

6. Herb Likens
7. Lowell Badger
8. Paul Ketner
9. Jerry Arburn
10. Arvel Borcherding

1993

1. Wayne Bode
2. Mike Zimmerman
3. Merlin Funk
4. Larry Boys
5. Rita Sharma
6. Herb Likens
7. Lowell Badger
8. Paul Ketner
9. Jerry Arburn
10. Arvel Borcherding

1994

1. Wayne Bode
2. Mike Zimmerman
3. Merlin Funk
4. Larry Boys
5. Rita Sharma
6. Herb Likens
7. Lowell Badger
8. Paul Ketner
9. Jerry Arburn
10. Arvel Borcherding

1995

1. Wayne Bode
2. Mike Zimmerman
3. Merlin Funk
4. Larry Boys
5. Rita Sharma
6. Herb Likens
7. Lowell Badger
8. Paul Ketner
9. Randy Kron*
10. Arvel Borcherding

*Elected mid-year following
Arburn's appointment as IFB
vice president July 1995.

1996

1. Wayne Bode
2. Mike Yoder

3. Merlin Funk
4. Larry Boys
5. Rita Sharma
6. Herb Likens
7. Lowell Badger
8. Paul Ketner
9. Randy Kron
10. Arvel Borcherding

1997

1. Wayne Bode
2. Mike Yoder
3. Merlin Funk
4. Larry Boys
5. Rita Sharma
6. Herb Likens
7. Don Villwock
8. Gary Reding
9. Randy Kron
10. George Corya

1998

1. Bob Herrold
2. Mike Yoder
3. Merlin Funk
4. Larry Boys
5. Rita Sharma
6. Herb Likens
7. Don Villwock*
8. Gary Reding
9. Randy Kron
10. George Corya

*Elected VP at December 1998
state convention)

1999

1. Bob Herrold
2. Mike Yoder
3. Merlin Funk
4. Carolyn Donson
5. Rita Sharma
6. Sheryl Fidler
7. Dale Brown*
8. Gary Reding
9. Randy Kron
10. George Corya

*Elected to Villwock's remain-
ing 1 year term.

America's Bicentennial (1776-1976) was celebrated in Indiana Farm Bureau's home office. Helping cut the cake were George Doup, IFB president; and Jack Roseborough, Farm Bureau Insurance companies chief executive officer.

Indiana Farm Bureau was the sponsor of this 12-horse hitch that made one of its appearances during the 1978 Farmers Day Parade. Membership exceeded 275,000 and was proudly displayed along with the parade theme, "Farm Power is Food Power."

B. Indiana Farm Bureau District Woman Leaders

District 1

Anna Moknes	1926-1930
Alice (P. C.) Womacks	1930-1954
Eacil (Edwin G.) Olson	1968-1978
Marie (Ray) Segert	1978-1987
Audrey (Charles) Zila	1987-1996
Joann (Wayne) Emigh	1996-

District 2

Prudence Ratts	1927-1930
Stella Goldsmith	1930-1938
(Morris) Hanson	1938-1941
Mildred (George) Neff	1941-1953
Lois (Guy E.) Gross	1953-1957
Pauline (George) Felger	1968-1973
Mildred (Ernest) Gross	1973-1979
Sharon (Richard) Strayer	1979-1988
Paula (Roger) Miller	1988-1994
Emily (Harold) Curie	1994 -

District 3

Bernice Humrickhouse	1926-1930
Ida M. Chenoweth	1930-1938
Mrs. Austin Cockran	1938-1944
Mrs. O.W. Stevens	1944-1947
Vivian (Jesse) Hoover	1947-1949
Mrs. Nelson Rupe	1949-1957
Blanche (James) Viney	1957-1969
Florence (Kenneth) Walters	1969-1984
Jeanette (Richard) McCabe	1984-1990
Eleanor Laffoon-Altepeter	1990-

District 4

Edith W. Mosley (appointed)	1922-1926
Marie McNeal	1926-1938
Lois Smith	1938-1949
Nora Bird	1949-1964
Freida Myers	1964-1976
Carolyn Hegel	1976-1980
Rosemary Crouch	1980-1988

Carolyn Donson	1988-1997
Kaye Kemper	1997- June 1998
Helen Witte	July 1998-

District 5

Mrs. George Neikirk	1926-
Mrs. Lawrence Foster	1927
Lillie Scott	1927-1938
Anna Crooks	1938-1964
Mable Herbert	1964-1974
Shirley Woody	1978-1987
Barbara Voyles	1987-1996
Joan Truax	1996-

District 6

Charlene Eliason	1927-
Mrs. Harry Modlin	1928-1929
Bessie Carpenter	1929-1936
Mrs. Russell Cushman	1936-1949
Lila Newman Bovard	1949-1951
Opal Swaim	1951-1961
Mary Etchison	1961-1973
Eleanora Matlock	1973-1985
Freida Painter	1985-1994
Sheryl Fidler	1994-1998
Donita Hiatt	1998-

District 7

Gussie Roberts	1926-1949
Zula Armstrong	1949-1957
Grace Fidler	1957-1977
Billie Simpson	1977-1986
Margaret Freeman	1986-1995
Ann Wilcoxen	1995-1998
Linda Hammelman	1998-

District 8

Grace Phendler	1927-1930
Mrs. Calvin Perdue	1930-1938
Nellie Flinn	1938-1948

Hazel Heck	1949-1977	Eleanor Uhde	1986-1993
Rita Yager	1977-1986	Erna Lloyd	1993-
Julia Bense	1986-1995		
Linda Bacon	1995-		

District 9

Grace Hanning	1926-1938
Della Robertson	?
Pina Taylor	?
Sybil Springer	1938-?
Anna Schwiersch	1948-1974
Eloise Michel	1974-1986

District 10

Mrs. C. L. Hill	1926-1930
Mrs. Edward Stegemoller	1930-1934
Irene Peters	1934-1939
Mrs. Goodwin	1939-1955
Ethel Mathias	1955-1966
Dorothy Hon	1966-1986
Lavonda Elliott	1986-1995
Wanda Kaiser	1995-

The traditional Farmers Day at the 1995 Indiana State Fair expanded with the addition of Machinery on Main Street. The six-hour open house allowed fair visitors to sit in a combine and see tractors, combines, planters and tillage equipment "up close and personal." Farmers were present to answer any consumer questions.

C. Indiana Farm Bureau Member Totals 1969–1999

Year	Associate	Voting	Total
1969	92,849	76,411	169,260
1970	111,418	76,293	187,711
1971	131,005	76,126	207,131
1972	138,735	77,684	216,419
1973	144,868	78,525	223,393
1974	142,579	80,834	223,413
1975	142,428	81,087	223,515
1976	157,438	82,687	240,125
1977	183,574	85,067	268,641
1978	196,155	86,587	282,742
1979	197,010	87,038	284,048
1980	189,980	86,428	276,408
1981	178,038	85,431	263,469
1982	172,381	83,915	256,296
1983	182,896	85,689	268,585
1984	179,568	82,682	262,250
1985	178,940	81,164	260,104
1986	184,188	81,313	265,501
1987	187,291	80,819	268,110
1988	192,546	82,630	275,176
1989	194,409	82,355	276,764
1990	167,418	79,918	247,336
1991	155,901	77,103	233,004
1992	157,308	76,569	233,877
1993	180,320	78,269	258,589
1994	191,944	79,021	270,965
1995	193,467	78,027	271,494
1996	190,929	80,699	271,628
1997	191,573	80,159	271,732
1998	192,807	79,611	272,418
1999	188,516	78,540	267,056

For many years district Farm Bureaus showcased local youth talent during the State Fair in the Farm Bureau Building. District 6 participants posed for a picture during the 1983 event.

Warrick County Ag Day was held at the local fairgrounds in 1991. Students got a first hand look at livestock and, for many, discovered where food originates.

Index

For many years Farm Bureau has provided welcome mats to Indiana's U.S. senators and representatives. During a visit in 1983, Don Henderson, right, IFB national affairs department director, presents a mat to Representative Dan Burton.

Viola Bangel, Marion County, was among countless volunteers that worked with Indiana Agricultural Marketing Association's cheese promotion, designed to increase sales of Agriculture Alumni mild cheddar & Colby cheeses and BodyRite, a low-fat/low-cholesterol swiss type cheese. A portion of sale proceeds was directed to Purdue University agricultural student scholarships.

9 781563 115264